Contents

PLACES

PEOPLE

White River Journal
RADIOBOOK

White River Journal
RADIOBOOK

Printed by
The Southwest Missouri State University
Printing Service
Springfield, Missouri

Library of Congress Catalog Card Number: 97-92325
ISBN: 0-9659309-0-4

Published by Public Radio Station KSMU

Illustrated by
Jeanne Stephens

Design by
Marty Sellmeyer and Brett Logan

EVENTS

Foreword
by Arlen Diamond
General Manager, KSMU

Bob Gilmore stopped by my office one day to talk about his interest in producing a series of historical programs for broadcast on KSMU. He was working with the White River Valley Historical Society to document interesting historical facts and stories which had their origins in or around the White River Valley in southwest Missouri and northwest Arkansas. I have known Bob for nearly two decades, since the day I visited with him while interviewing for the position of radio station manager and assistant professor of speech at Southwest Missouri State University. So, I knew that when Bob volunteered to produce the White River Journal radio series as a labor of love, something great would emerge. I was not mistaken.

The White River Journal series has been a fascinating look back into the history of the Ozarks. Bob has brought to life parades, fistfights, and paddle wheelers on the White River, all a part of life which we, today, are enriched by knowing. The radio series was a wonderful addition to KSMU's program schedule. Fortunately, though, the value of the programs did not end with their broadcast.

One day last year, Bob brought by the station the scripts of some of his programs. He thought they might make a nice book and he wanted me to read them. I couldn't put them down. His stories were as compelling on the printed page as they were on the radio. And so, a book was born. Once again, Bob Gilmore set out to produce something, not for money or for personal recognition, but because it was important to do. This book is the result of his efforts.

My life has been enriched by my association with Bob. I've enjoyed his keen insight, his sharp mind, his quick and humorous retorts. It has been a pleasure to work for and with him over the years. This, truly, is among the best productions of his life. I am pleased that he chose KSMU as the vehicle for the radio programs and as his partner for the publication of the book. But then, working with Bob is easy—he does all the heavy lifting.

Preface and Acknowledgments

This *RadioBook* is a collection of short essays, or more precisely radio scripts, that have been broadcast as *White River Journal* over KSMU.

A journal, according to my dictionary, is a record of occurrences, experiences, and observations. Fact and fancy, memories and current happenings, opinions and ideas, all found their way into the *Journals*. Some *Journals* reflect the long ago, others the right now. I've tried to explore people, places, and events from all over our part of the Missouri and Arkansas Ozarks.

White River is a proud name for an Ozarks Journal. Its flow is interrupted now by four great man-made lakes, but over eons, the White River created for itself a scenic Ozarks domain, carving great bluffs, tracing graceful meander loops, and forming broad valleys. The river rises from a spring branch in Northwest Arkansas and makes its way in a great bend through southwest Missouri before again flowing south and joining the Mississippi in southeastern Arkansas, 720 miles from its source.

The White River was always an important highway into the Ozarks. The Native Americans were here first, of course, followed by hunters and trappers. Then early settlers came up the great river highway, seeking land on which they could build a home, develop a farmstead, rear a family and earn a livelihood. Woods and water were important, and the Ozarks had lots of both. Forests, lakes, and streams continue to be important to the Ozarks, not only in making a living but in the quality of our lives.

Bowing to the time tyranny of radio, these essays are all exactly the same length– the number of words that can be read aloud in six minutes. Let this uniformity remind you that each *Journal* was written to be heard– the cadence of the spoken word is slightly different from that of the written word. Consider this a suggestion. You may want to read some of these scripts aloud, especially those which have other voices in them, as when other people are interviewed.

I hope you enjoy reading, or hearing, these journals as much as I have enjoyed preparing and broadcasting them. Special thanks are due to Arlen Diamond and Mike Smith of KSMU for the opportunity they have provided; to Barbara Wehrman and *The Ozarks Mountaineer* for their sponsorship; and to the White River Valley Historical Society, especially Lynn Morrow and Linda Myers-Phinney, for much good historical data and excellent ideas.

Robert K. Gilmore

PLACES

"Float lightly, speed swiftly and safely!

Long live the Queen!"

Steamboats on the White River

Dockhands are casting off the lines, and the Captain sounds a long, low, mournful blast on the ship's horn. Tourists have already boarded the Branson Belle at White River Landing on Table Rock Lake. They will soon be steaming, or rather dieseling, down the lake, dining, being entertained by a musical show, and admiring the spring lake side scenery. The Branson Belle is the latest, and certainly the largest, paddlewheel boat to ply the waters of the White River.

Most of us know that canoes and keel boats came up the White River in the early days, bringing hunters and trappers, and later settlers into our area. But you may be surprised, as I was, at the number of steamboats that used that river for over a hundred years.

There were at least 422 of them— beginning with the Waverly, The Laurel, and the Bob Handy in 1831 and ending with the Mary Woods in 1933. I know all this because I read it in a fine new book, *Steamboats and Ferries on White River,* which has recently been published by the University of Central Arkansas Press. One of the authors is Pat Wood:

> *I had no idea, even though I grew up here, that there were so many steamboats on the White River. The first one was in 1831, and they continued into the 1930s.*

Steamboat travel up the White River was a way of connecting the isolated Ozarks with the larger outside world. Pat Wood explains:

> *Actually, there is a natural division on the White River at Jackson Port, Arkansas. The river from there to the mouth is quite wide and sandy, so deep water boats could literally come there year round from*

*New Orleans, Memphis, St. Louis, even as far away as Louisville. And
then at Jackson Port the cargo, or passengers, was shifted over to
smaller steamboats that came up as far as Lead Hill quite frequently,
and several came to Forsyth fairly regularly, with two going as far as
the mouth of the James River. So they, during the 1800s, were really a
primary mode of carrying cargo and to an extent passengers too, into
this area.*

The steamboats hauled a great variety of freight, including bear oil, says co-
author Sammie Rose:

*There were a lot of bear in this country. And there were rendering
plants. In fact, Oil Trough, Arkansas got its name due to rendering
bear oil. They would haul out a tree and fill it with bear oil and then
it would set up, you know, when it was cool, and they could ship the
oil thataway.*

*(Pat Wood) And lots of cotton, lots of cotton went out. And tobacco.
Of course hogs were a big one, beef to an extent, lumber's always
been big—you name it, they hauled it out of here.*

(Sammie Rose) They also shipped a lot of wild game.

*(Pat Wood) And then into the area they carried furniture, and the
things that were staples—sugar, flour, gunpowder, whisky, sugar, and
salt—basics, the things that everyone needed.*

It's not surprising that the steam boats that used the upper White River had shallow drafts:

*(Sammie Rose) In fact, one of the captains made the statement that his
boat had such a shallow draft that it could run on a heavy dew.
Another one said that if the water was a little low, a mere spit would
elevate the water to a level that he could run on it.*

*(Pat Wood) They usually had a draft of two, two and a half feet.
Those boats could literally be jumped over...you know the White
River is famous for its shoals. A boat that needed two and a half feet,
they could jump it over a two foot shoal by cordelling to a tree on the
bank, and then they would tie it up taut to a whip lift on the boat, put
it in reverse to push the water under the boat, and jerk her forward*

just a hair. Then do the whole process again.

Steamboats and Ferries On White River is a handsome book, well written and researched, and with a wealth of historic steamboat pictures. Sammie Rose and Pat Wood share authorship credit with Duane Huddleston, who died in 1982. "He left a lasting legacy of historical research," they write in their acknowledgements. "It has been a joy to incorporate his writings with ours." The book also has lots of good information about the many ferries that served White River:

> *(Pat Wood) They were here prior to the steamboat's appearance. And because they were established sites, many of them became steamboat landings as well, so the ferries were really interchangeable with the steamboats to some extent.*

In September, 1896, at the Batesville, Arkansas landing, a brand new stern-wheeler was about to begin her service. A local girl, little June Glenn, pronounced the words: "I christen thee Ozark Queen. Glide smoothly to thy home on the beautiful White. Float lightly, speed swiftly and safely! Long live the Queen."

With that she shattered a bottle containing sparkling White River water against the bow of the steamboat.

Almost a hundred years later, in April 1995, entertainer Kenny Rogers christened the Branson Belle, saying, "I christen thee showboat Branson Belle." He then smashed against her bow a hand-blown flask containing water carefully collected from Table Rock Lake—from a spot directly above the old White River channel.

"Long live the Queen!" "Long live the Belle!" And long live the steamships and ferries of White River.

For early Ozarkers, "going to mill" was

both a necessity and a pleasure.

Grist Mills

One gorgeous May day, a month or so ago, I told my wife I had some work to do. I needed to do some "field research," I told her. Soon I found myself, hard at work, driving through our beautiful Ozarks hills, on my way to visit a place that is not as well known today as it was, say, a hundred years ago. Had I made the trip a hundred years ago, I would have told my wife I was "going to mill."

For early Ozarkers, "going to mill" was both a necessity and a pleasure. Farmers needed to take in their corn and wheat and oats to have it ground into cornmeal and flour for their own use, and into feed for their livestock. But they would often bring the wife and kids along and while they were waiting their turn at the mill, the whole family could visit with seldom-seen friends, catch up on news, fish in the mill pond, pitch horseshoes, exchange recipes, and just in general enjoy a break from their usual hardworking and lonely existence.

I was going to mill, not in a wagon or on muleback, but in my trusty Ford Festiva. In Douglas county I was visiting Topaz, a name not found on today's road maps. Going to Topaz today is, to say the least, to get off the beaten path. You take a county road for a while until the blacktop ends, then keep going on the gravel and dirt road for a mile or two, bearing right, until you reach the North Fork River, and the Topaz mill. When the mill was first built, just a hundred years ago, it was not so isolated. It didn't take long for a small hamlet to grow up around the mill. Owner Joe O'Neal explains:

> *The store and the mill was here, and it was more or less just a trading*
> *center for, say, about a 20 mile area around here where the people*
> *came and bought their produce—brought their produce in to have it*

processed into meal and flour. They came to the general store to get
all their supplies. There was a post office. The general area here was
called the Topaz post office.

The mill builder and owner, a man named Robartus—or Bart—Hutcheson, also built a cannery and a blacksmith shop. He even had a barbershop in a small shed room of the mill itself. Hutcheson died before he could complete plans to build a bank. His widow continued to operate the mill until the 1930s, and the general store until 1945. The general store, by the way, still stands. It's a substantial structure, and its balcony, showcases, and shelves are still intact.

Although the mill is on the banks of the upper North Fork river, it is powered by water from a spring which produces about 8 to 10 million gallons per day. Hutcheson built a dam and created a spring-fed mill pond. A flume directed water from the mill pond to turn the turbine which powered the machinery.

The mill built by Hutcheson in 1895 was not the first at this site. A Choctaw Indian woman named Alabeth Freeman and her husband Aaron had acquired the property and built a small mill there about 1840. It was powered directly by the waters from the spring, and would have been considerably smaller than Hutcheson's structure. There may have been other mills at the spring before Hutcheson's very substantial structure was built. A good mill site is a good mill site.

People who know about these things think that by 1880 there were probably 900 mills in the state of Missouri. Lots of these were in the Ozarks because of the many springs and free-flowing streams that provided an ample source of water power. Also, because the rugged landscape made it difficult to get around in the Ozarks, mills tended to be built closer together, so a farmer wouldn't have to travel quite so far with his corn or wheat. Hodgson mill and Zanoni, for example, in Ozark County, south of Topaz, are only about five miles apart. Both of these mills, by the way, were developed by their owners into hamlets. Each had a store, blacksmith shop, cotton gin, and a post office.

I know the term "heritage" is overused sometimes. But the watermills of the Ozarks, and the hamlets that grew up around them, are part of our past—our heritage—that is going to be gone, forgotten, and difficult to explain to our children if something isn't done.

Fortunately, something is being done. People and groups who care are making efforts to maintain many of our mills. When I asked Joe O'Neal why he was working to preserve and restore his mill at Topaz, he sounded surprised that I should have to ask:

> Well, I've got quite of an interest in the old mills. My father was a
> miller for years and years, and it's just something I'd like for the
> future generations to be able to see down the line somewhere.

With luck—and a generous supply of dedication, hard work, and funding— maybe Topaz and many more of our beautiful Ozarks gristmills will be available for people to see down the line somewhere. I hope we can all continue "going to mill" for generations to come.

"The Creator did not see fit to make the first man

a merchant or a manufacturer, or a banker or a

lawyer or a railroad president or a miner or a

mechanic or a trust magnate, or a printer or a

preacher. He started the world with a farmer.

Ash Grove is a farming community.

Our people are of the best."

State Normal School Number Four

There was a lot of excitement in southwest Missouri in the spring of 1905. In March of that year, the State Legislature had authorized the establishment of two new Normal Schools. One of these, the Fourth District Normal School, was to be built in some fortunate community in southwest Missouri.

Springfield, of course, was eventually selected as the site of the new Fourth District School, and it is difficult now to imagine the institution that would eventually become Southwest Missouri State University located elsewhere. But in early 1905 there were at least 12 southwest Missouri communities convinced that they should be the location of this center of learning. One of these was Ash Grove.

The campaign to attract the new school to that northwest Greene County town was led by J. O. Waddle, the aggressive editor of the weekly newspaper, *The Commonwealth*. Editor Waddle was never timid about expressing in print his opinions on any matter that caught his attention. And for years *The Commonwealth* carried on its masthead the modest slogan, "The Official Organ of the World."

The opening round in the campaign for the new Normal school was fired by editor Waddle in a *Commonwealth* article on April 20, 1905. In a style that would be perfectly familiar to anyone following presidential primary races, he started by listing all the negative factors of the other communities seeking the school. Springfield is a "whiskey town," he charged, with "more drinking places than dry goods stores."

Greenfield, he allowed graciously, "is a pretty fair town," but has only a "little jerkwater" train. "You couldn't reach it from anywhere in a week or 12 days."

Webb City is dismissed as only a "mining camp." "Let its mines fail and it would vanish from the map." And as for Neosho, "Where is Neosho anyway? . . Never saw anybody who had ever been there or would ever go there."

That left, of course, Ash Grove, with all its attributes. Unlike Greenfield, Ash Grove is situated on a main line railroad, the Frisco, in the heart of "the best agricultural district in this section of the state." This town, he bragged, "has more cultured people within its borders than any town of its size within 300 miles."

And in sharp contrast to neighboring Springfield, "We are a town of churches and no saloons," introducing an argument that was to be repeated and expanded upon many times in the ensuing campaign.

The community took on a theological emphasis. "The Creator did not see fit to make the first man a merchant or a manufacturer, or a banker or a lawyer or a railroad president or a miner or a mechanic or a trust magnate, or a printer or a preacher, " the editor stated. "He started the world with a farmer. Ash Grove is in a farming community. Our people are of the best."

A local lady followed up on this theme. "Parents need have no fear in sending their boys and girls to Ash Grove, that they should fall into bad company or find too many distracting attractions to entice them away from their school work." And, she assured parents, "There are no saloons and public sentiment is so strong against saloon license that there will never be one in this generation."

Over the next several weeks, *The Commonwealth* continued to list the advantages of Ash Grove as a site for the new Normal School. The good railroad passenger service, the cultural opportunities, the benefits of a small community, the healthfulness of the climate and the water, and the large number of churches were all cited. As was, of course, the absence of any saloons.

The Normal School would be of great benefit to the community, it was pointed out, especially for economic reasons. "Students are great eaters," a correspondent wrote, and they would create "a greater demand for goods in the stores." Many of the visitors to the School, from friends and parents of the students to members of the legislature and the State Board of Education, would be so taken by the community that they would become permanent residents.

Well, we all know Springfield won the bidding war for State Normal School Number 4—$25,000 cash and any site which the Commission might select. Editor Waddle conceded the loss with a gracious editorial saying that "Since

Ash Grove didn't get the Normal School proposition, we are glad to see that the institution goes to Springfield."

"The Official Organ of the World" and its irrepressible editor had not won this particular campaign, but there were other challenges in view. An electric railroad from near the state line west of Nevada to Springfield, passing through Ash Grove, for example. "Ash Grove cannot and must not let this opportunity pass…"

He spent quite a bit of his time, he told me,

caring for several Griffin graves in the cemetery,

including the plot where he would be buried.

Buffalo River Country

In August, I spent several days in the Buffalo River country of Arkansas. I wanted to explore, not the river itself, but some of the places along the river that have been part of the rich heritage of this beautiful and rugged country.

I'm sorry! I didn't even make it into the second paragraph before using the word "rugged." Seems like everybody who talks or writes about Buffalo River Country has to use the word. My computer's thesaurus lists some alternatives— "craggy," "jagged," "rough," "stony," "uneven.". Those words are also quite appropriate. I'll probably be using one or more of them before I'm through. I'll try not to say "rugged" again.

To get anywhere in the Buffalo River valley you go down. Over eons the river has cut itself a deep and narrow path through the Arkansas hills on its way to join the White River. Most roads in Arkansas follow ridgetops, with an occasional dip into a valley before they climb back to the ridge again. The dip into the Buffalo River valley is always a significant, gear-busting, brake- riding drop before you cross the river and begin the long climb back up again.

You get to Snowball, Arkansas, by crossing the Buffalo on highway 65, going down, then back up, continuing a few miles south, and then turning right on state highway 74. Snowball is on Calf Creek, a tributary of the Buffalo. In August, Calf Creek was a mere trickle, but there were many signs that it becomes a robust stream in other seasons.

I drove through the small ghost village. No store, gas station, or cafe was open for business. I noted that almost every building in town had a tin roof. I wandered through the very neat, well- tended cemetery on the north edge of town. Two small grave-stones caught my attention. "Infant son of J. B. and I. C.

Griffin," one read. He had died in August, 1909, aged two months. The other stone carried a poignantly similar inscription "Born July 5, 1910, Died July 7, 1910." The parents' graves were alongside.

Still thinking about the hurt those parents must have suffered, losing two infant children within a year, I approached an elderly gentleman tending some graves at the upper end of the small cemetery. We howdied and talked about a number of things, including why all the buildings had tin roofs, and how Snowball got its name.

Well, he allowed, a salesman had come through and sold one family a tin roof, and everybody liked it, so one after another, when their roofs started leaking, they just replaced them with tin.

What about the name?

The community was originally known as Calf Creek, it seems. When the Masons built a lodge in town about 1887, they wanted to honor one of their active members, "Uncle Ben" Snow. They asked the Postal Service in Washington to rename the town, "Snow Hall." Perhaps the writing in their petition was unclear, but approval came back for "Snowball," and so it has been.

My informant, I learned, was Mr. Fred Griffin, a younger brother to the two infants whose graves I had noticed earlier. He spent quite a bit of his time, he told me, caring for several Griffin graves in the cemetery, including the plot where he would be buried.

There are only a few families living in Snowball now, Mr. Griffin told me, but in earlier times it was quite a bustling place, with a hotel, seven or eight stores, a cotton gin, two grist mills, a sawmill, and a school, in addition to the Masonic Hall—Mr. Snow's Hall.

"Come see me," Mr. Griffin said as I left. "I live just past the low water bridge on the right. I'm home most of the time now." I went back through the tin roofs of Snowball and drove west for a way on a graveled county road, past the burned-out rock remains of the school. I would have liked to go all the way to Richland Valley over Rollins Mountain, through McCutcheon Gap, and the ford at Richland Creek but I was afraid my car didn't have the clearance needed for either the road or the ford, so I turned back.

Suzie Rogers is the historian at the Buffalo National River in Harrison,

Arkansas. She calls the Buffalo River Valley a "place of the heart" to those who have known it. It nurtured pioneer settlers in snug coves and sheltered valleys, she goes on, "where the fabric of life was pieced together, like a well loved quilt, among a known group of family and friends."

There were many "places of the heart"in Buffalo River Country. Places like Gilbert, Rush, and Boxley Valley, Ponca, and the Parker—Hickman Farmstead.

We'll visit some of them in a later White River Journal.

"It has had very, very few alterations through the years. The state of the house itself, although it needs a considerable amount of stabilization and rehabilitative work on some of its elements, was largely unchanged through the years."

Nathan Boone Homestead Historic Site

Boone County, Boonville, Boonsboro, Boones Lick—these are all familiar Missouri place names marking the legacy of a celebrated family. Not so well known, perhaps, is a new addition to the Boone tradition—the Nathan Boone Homestead State Historic Site in Greene County, just north of Ash Grove.

Nathan was the tenth child and youngest son of the famous frontiersman, Daniel Boone. He was only 18 when he came to Missouri with his 16 year old bride, Olive. Carole Bills lives at Ash Grove and has researched the life of Nathan Boone. He was quite resourceful, Carole says.

Once he traded a saddle and a bridle worth $120 for 680 acres of land and began to make a home for Olive.

He was an experienced trapper and hunter.

He and a friend once trapped 900 beavers and sold the pelts to trappers in Lexington, Kentucky, for $2.50 apiece.

Nathan manufactured salt with his brother, Daniel Morgan, at the salt springs in central Missouri now known as the Boone's Lick State Historic Site. During the War of 1812, he became a commissioned officer in a ranger company, and served about three years. He prospered in St. Charles County, and served as a delegate to the Constitutional Convention held in St. Louis in 1820. Then in 1832, at age 51, he reentered the army where he served for the next 20 years. After retiring because of his health, he spent the last three years of his life with Olive at their home in Greene County. Carole Bills says,

I'm sure people wonder how he happened to come to Ash Grove. Well Nathan had to sell the beautiful three-story house that he and his father built in St. Charles County when he had to pay the debt of a

friend for whom he was bondsman. And it's believed that Nathan had passed through what is now Greene County while surveying Indian Territory, and he liked what he saw. So in 1835 he sent three sons to preempt 1200 acres of land in Greene County.

What Nathan built on this land was a double pen, dogtrot log house. That is, two log boxes, about 17 feet square, separated by a central hallway, or "dogtrot." The whole is covered by one roof. The house was originally sided with hand riven walnut clapboards. There is a veranda on the side of the house facing the creek.

Booker Rucker, with the State Parks and Historic Sites program in Jefferson City, tells why the Department of Natural Resources was pleased to be able to acquire the property in 1991:

The place in Greene County is especially interesting because it has had very, very few alterations through the years. The state of the house itself, although it needs a considerable amount of stabilization and rehabilitative work on some of its elements, was largely unchanged through the years. No one who lived there remodeled it or impacted heavily on it, so when visitors are allowed to see it, you're going to see that the original woodwork, the original doors, all the hand- made elements to it have been preserved more or less intact all through the years.

Some archaeological work on the homestead site has been completed, but more needs to be done to discover more features of the property as they were in Nathan's time.

Rucker is pleased that the Parks and Historic Sites people were able to acquire 370 acres of the original Nathan Boone farm.

The setting of it is remarkable in that we have very few opportunities to preserve things with context. And the Boone House at Ash Grove is particularly of interest because there are hundreds of acres of rolling prairie land around it that have never been built upon. The house sits naturally on the land, in a bit of a bowl or depression...When the house is restored and is open to the public, when you're at the house, you won't see anything much different than what Nathan saw when he

sat on his own porch, which is mainly a view of the prairie land
around it.

When will the site be open to the public? No firm time for the completion of the restoration of the house has been set, but the Parks people hope to get a temporary road and parking facilities in soon, so, as Booker Rucker says, people can come in and stroll the grounds, visit the family grave sites, and just look around and satisfy their curiosity as to what's there.

Carole Bills says that her research convinces her that Nathan was a worthy son of his more illustrious father. And she takes satisfaction in knowing that after losing his fine home and property in St. Charles County, and devoting most of his life to military service, he did, indeed, finally prosper:

They brought their slaves with them, they had cattle, they had fruit
trees. They had a fruit cellar. You know, it's still there. And so by
standards in Greene County, he became a wealthy man again.

"We have blue stem grass here that would grow,

especially on these glades, would grow as high as

a horse's back and that was the best grass ever

was in the state of Missouri, or the United States,

is that ole blue stem grass."

"The land will make you a living
if you let it."

When Ellen Massey's "Bittersweet" students interviewed Warren Cook in 1978, this Republic, Missouri farmer told them, "The land will make you a living if you let it."

Now I live on a Stone County, Missouri ridge top. The deed says we have 12 acres, but the house and garden and a side yard occupy about an acre and a half. The rest of that 12 acres is straight up and down, and covered with timber and rock. With all due respect to Mr. Cook, I'd sure hate to count on my 12 acres making me a living. How did people in earlier times make their living from this thin-soiled, rocky, hilly country? Denver Hollars described it best when he said:

They didn't live to get rich down there, they lived just to survive.

Denver was talking about the people who lived in the Dogwood Canyon area on Little Indian Creek and Dogwood Creek, in extreme southern Stone County, Missouri.

The narrow valleys of Dogwod and Little Indian Creeks didn't lend themselves to large scale crop farming, but they would support a few families who could employ all their members in a diversified subsistence lifestyle— raising some crops, planting a garden, running some livestock, and working in the timber, as well as hunting, trapping, and fishing.

Sometimes they'd have some little bottoms there, that would have a
pretty good little patch of corn in 'em, and there were some sawmills
up there. They'd cut that butternut timber up there and they'd gather
the pawpaws and black haws, winter grapes and besides all the
mushrooms, they had quite a living up there. And all that water, and
all the things that grow up in there, in them little bottoms, they was

alivin' pretty good in them days.

Denver was born on the banks of the King's River in Arkansas in 1904. For over 65 years he has lived on a farm just north of Dogwood Canyon. He has an excellent memory and a fine sense of history. His description of the lifestyles of the people who lived in and around the Dogwood Canyon provides a remarkable insight into the way the land, even this rugged Ozarks land, can be made to give up a living.

> *Others lived as truck farmers. They'd farm down there. They growed*
> *their own potatoes, they growed their beans, and they growed enough*
> *corn to grind their own meal...*

There was trapping, of course—for mink, beaver, coon, possum, fox, rabbits, and other game. These pelts represented one of the few sources of cash money for the early settlers.

Hogs were the livestock of choice.

> *And they grew hogs and fattened 'em out on the acorns. And maybe*
> *they finished 'em up on a bushel or two of corn and they eat what was*
> *called acorn fattened hogs. Which was about the best meat you ever*
> *eat, it was just a little softer—little softer than corn-fed, because corn*
> *fed meat was much solider and firmer than the acorn hogs.*

I examined an 1876 Stone County census which showed that corn was the predominant crop—more than eight times more bushels of corn were grown than either wheat or oats.

I found it interesting that this same census reveals no—absolutely *no*— whiskey or wine in all of Stone County in 1876. I wonder. Is it possible that these early Stone County residents might have failed to respond in a completely accurate way when a census-taker asked about the family stock of alcohol? There are many authorities who believe that Ozarkers marketed their corn crop in two ways—by the bushel and by the gallon.

Clearing the land, for any kind of crop, in the days before bulldozers was no easy task:

> *All we had was a chopping ax and a cross cut saw. Then a lot of*
> *timber when we cleared it we just used a chopping ax and ringed it,*
> *sort of cut the sap all the way around it, and it would die. And then it*

would fall down eventually, and then in four or five years it would be pretty well cleaned up.

Even the landscape was different.

We have blue stem grass here that would grow, especially on these glades, would grow as high as a horse's back and that was the best grass ever was in the state of Missouri, or the United States, is that ole blue stem grass. Back in them days we had what we called open range, where you turned your cattle loose and they'd go for miles, graze off that blue stem grass.

Dogwood Canyon is a reminder of the splendid isolation in which many early Ozarkers lived while struggling to wring a living from the grudging land. To survive, these families, as in many parts of the Ozarks, made use of every natural resource available to them—the soil, the timber, the wildlife, the water.

When Warren Cook said, "The land will make you a living if you let it," I don't think he was suggesting to these young people that the land was there, like money in the bank, drawing interest and providing income to the owners with no further effort on their parts. "Unearned" income, economists would call it.

Few Ozarkers who have ever depended on the land for a living would call their income unearned.

"They came to the area because of its outdoor beauty. And they came to get away from the city, and to recall an earlier, supposedly simpler kind of life, a more balanced life. And I think that is still what Branson offers to the city dweller."

Branson Tourism

Every once in awhile I get to thinking about the millions of visitors coming into the Branson area each year, and wondering if the heritage of the White River Valley area is playing any kind of a role in this touristic phenomenon. I decided to ask someone who would know.

Jessica Howard is a graduate student in performance studies at New York University. For about a year she lived in the Branson area, doing research for her doctoral dissertation about performance aspects of the Branson development.

She's also been getting acquainted with the people and the area, talking to tourists, going to shows, taking notes, observing, studying our history—doing all the things a good researcher needs to do. I thought Jessica would be a good person to talk to for an informed outsider's opinion about what's happening in Branson. In particular, I was interested in her views about the way our traditional culture fits into this whole mix.

I asked if part of this culture involved our traditional country music.

Country music, what became known as country music, derived primarily from ballads and various kinds of fiddle and instrumental music from the old world—from England, Scots-Irish traditions, that sort of thing. But once it came to the United States, it became influenced by many other things. Specifically, popular entertainment that traveled, African-American traditions, religious music, gospel music, and the music that came out of the great awakening. All these things combined to produce the kind of music that ultimately ended up on early country radio.

By the late 1940s, she believes, most traditional country music, not only in the Ozarks, but in other regions of the United States as well, had been pretty well homogenized by nation wide country radio.

> *And in the '60s when you started seeing country performances as part of Branson's tourist offerings, it was the kind of music you heard on country radio, and was not necessarily particular to this area.*

Early country radio had an effect on many of today's Branson stage productions—even the patriotic numbers featured in many shows can be traced back to old time country radio.

> *Almost all early country radio shows had overtly patriotic numbers and certainly Protestant religion expressions as well. So in that sense Branson's not really doing anything new, it's plugging into a formula that worked 40-plus years ago. And that in itself helps with the nostalgia aspect.*

From the very beginning , Jessica says, two important factors have drawn visitors to Branson the scenery and nostalgia:

> *They came to the area because of its outdoor beauty. And they came to get away from the city, and to recall an earlier, supposedly simpler kind of life, a more balanced life. And I think that is still what Branson offers to the city dweller.*

For many visitors, Jessica says, coming to Branson is like coming home. Or at least to the way home ought to be.

> *Branson certainly markets itself as that kind of destination. The kind of America that used to be—supposedly that was a safe and happy place. That was a place involving religion, involving family, involving patriotism, and things that many people feel are in crisis today. And when they come to Branson they feel like they're coming back to the fold, which is nation and nature, and they feel...they feel good about themselves.*

The music shows along 76 Country Boulevard and nearby locations are obviously very attractive to visitors. What accounts for their success? Jessica responds by quoting a prominent Branson entertainer:

> *Box Car Willy claims that what is happening in Branson today is nothing more than old time vaudeville with the different segments*

*more modernized. With more familiar music, and this sort of thing. It's
hard to believe that someone like Andy Williams is practicing
vaudeville, but he's a television variety show host, as are a number of
others in town, and so a variety format, which is a very, very old
format, is being used. And like I say, the patriotic elements, the
religious elements, are all part of early country radio, and I think
have an old-time quality to them.*

Country music has always been simultaneously folk and commercial, Jessica
explained. The earlier music has been modified by popular entertainment
traditions. The result, she says, is that it's quite difficult to separate what is true,
or pure, from what has been commercialized.

I guess that sounds a lot like Branson. Branson certainly has been
commercialized, no argument. But much of its success has been based on what
many of us like to think of as the real thing—our own culture and traditions,
and by its location in this beautiful place we call the Ozarks.

Had the river been dammed, Gilbert might today

be the Branson of Lake Buffalo.

Arkansas Odyssey

In an earlier White River Journal we visited Snowball, Arkansas. Let's continue this Arkansas Odyssey.

Gilbert and Mull, two Buffalo River communities I visited in August, had developed and flourished in the early part of this century, each in its own unique way.

Today, the homes of the 43 permanent residents of Gilbert, Arkansas, are neat and well-tended. Mrs. Lucille Baker and Mr. Leon Shipman have both lived in Gilbert most of their lives, and graciously invited me into their homes and shared their knowledge of the village with me.

Gilbert is a little bit east of highway 65, just before you come to the Buffalo River. Although it's right on the river, Gilbert was a railroad town—a bustling commercial hub for the Buffalo River valley. It was formed and planned by the Missouri and North Arkansas Railroad around the turn of the century, and named for the railroad superintendent, F. A. Gilbert.

In its heyday, I learned, Gilbert boasted a big Eagle pencil factory, tie yards, cattle pens, two hotels, a cotton gin, and a number of stores. The saloon, sad to say, was washed away in a flood in 1915.

In the early 1920s, the population of Gilbert increased dramatically when members of a millennialist sect from Illinois moved in. Before the millenium could begin, the sect's leader taught, there must be a world wide war between Catholics and Protestants. To survive this holocaust, followers were to establish communities in isolated mountainous regions of the country, and work to restore the true church.

One of these communities was established at Gilbert. The official newspaper,

The Kingdom Harbinger, was printed and distributed nationwide from Gilbert. The new church people were very industrious, I was told, and blended in quite well with the local citizens. After about 1925, however, interest in the religious experiment faded, and many of the colonists left.

Today, Gilbert is a popular put-in for those floating the Buffalo. A different role might have been in store for the town, had the U.S. Corps of Engineers had its way. Back in the 1950s and 60s, the Engineers were proposing a high dam to be erected across the Buffalo, just a few miles upstream from Gilbert. Had the river been dammed, Gilbert might today be the Branson of Lake Buffalo.

You won't find Dillard's Ferry on the Arkansas State Highway map, nor will you find Mull. But if you drive down highway 14, about 14 miles south of Yellville there will be a road sign proclaiming the community of Mull. Keep going, and a high bridge will take you over the Buffalo River. Earlier in this century, you would have taken the ferry across the river, the ferry operated by J. F. (Doc) Dillard and his boys.

The Yellville *Mountain Echo* in the early 1930s described the empire ruled over by Doc Dillard. "No government by a patriarch told in sacred or profane history was more perfect than life in the Dillard settlement for half a century," proclaimed the *Echo*.

The settlement included a store, saw mill, lumber industry, grist mill, sorghum mill and other small community enterprises. All of these were directed by the patriarch of the settlement, 'Doc' Dillard, for the benefit of his children and grandchildren.

Each of the fourteen children born to the Dillards had his or her place in the community. "No socialistic community," the *Echo* said, "could be more perfectly and fairly managed for the benefit of all than was the Dillard settlement. All disputes were settled by the patriarch. His word was law."

For years the area was isolated from the outside world. Yet, the *Mountain Echo* reported, "For more than a third of a century lumber from the Dillard saw mill went out by wagon to Yellville, Marshall, and other towns on the railroad or went by boat or raft down the Buffalo."

Mrs. Doretha Dillard Shipman is a grandaughter of Doc Dillard. I visited with her and her husband Leon in their pleasant, shaded, rambling house not far from the Dillard Settlement acreage where she was born and raised.

"My grandparents had 14 children," she told me over cups of coffee, "and I always wanted to have 14 children too." Did you make your goal?, I wondered. "Yes, I did," she replied. "I had seven children and they each married, and there are the 14." Those 14, and a number of grandchildren, crowd the Shipman's spacious farm house after church just about every Sunday.

Before I left, Mrs. Shipman filled up my coffee cup again and asked if I wouldn't eat a hot ham sandwich. As she placed it in front of me she said, somewhat apologetically, that the only thing she had to make the sandwich with was a "flat biscuit." The flat biscuit turned out to be two slices of store-bought bread.

It was delicious.

"The people are the 'Hill Folks,' jovial, sociable,

and appreciable. Turn your car this way—Ozark

will welcome you cordially and you will leave

with the intent of coming again."

Getting to Ozark

Before we moved down to Stone County a couple of years ago, to the Reeds Spring community, my wife and I lived just outside Ozark, the County Seat of Christian County, Missouri.

It was easy to tell our friends in Springfield how to get to Ozark. "It's on highway 65, about 12 miles south" we'd say, sometimes adding, "on the way to Branson." Ozark is just a 15 minute breeze from the Queen City on a four-lane divided highway. "Just stay on highway 65."

Directions to Ozark were not always so simple. In earlier times roads were not as well marked as they are now, nor were they nearly as direct. A trip to anywhere, even Ozark, required very specific directions. If you were a motorist in 1925 you would do well to take along a tourist guide, such as the Loumar Log, to help you reach your destination.

The Loumar Log's directions to Ozark began on the east side of the public square in Springfield, at mile 00.0. "Go east on St. Louis Street," you were directed, "follow Log No. 5A to mile 09.1."

At 09.1, you were then told, the "Road forks. Straight ahead with right fork, following State Highway markers No. 3."

At 09.9 you "jog right, then left." "Straight ahead" at mile 10.3, but a little later, you're cautioned, "Avoid road on left."

It's routine for awhile, some curve rights, more straight aheads, a jog left, then right.

The Log gets your attention at mile 15.2 with a capitalized, boldfaced "CAUTION—Slow down—long, steep down grade." And again at 15.7, "Sound horn for blind curve on down grade."

At 16.3 you go "under the railroad trestle, then bear right, up grade." Watch carefully now—you turn left, then at the next corner, right. And you have finally reached Ozark, the "Northwest corner of the Square. Ozark Drug Store on corner on left. Appetite Cafe. Courthouse in middle of square."

I asked Connie Todd, who has an office on the Square in Ozark, to share what else the Loumar guide book had to say about the Ozark of 1925:

> Ozark is an oasis in the heart of the Ozark Mountains on the banks of the classic little Finley River. With a population of about 1,000 it has light, water, and sewer systems, four churches, three banks, two hotels, and business houses that would do credit to a town much larger. A $100,000 Court House of brick and stone, a $50,000 fire proof high school building (12 grades). A branch road of the Frisco gives good train service. It is 17.7 miles southeast of Springfield, Missouri, 45 minutes by auto on the graded hard-surface state highway.
> The people are the "Hill Folks," jovial, sociable, and appreciable.
> Turn your car this way—Ozark will welcome you cordially and you will leave with the intent of coming again.

The purpose of this little venture into nostalgia is twofold: first, to remind us that "the good old days" probably never were as good as we remember them, or as they look in the movies. That trip to Ozark in 1925 might have been exciting, but it sure wasn't very comfortable. The Loumar people didn't mention the rocks and chugholes all along the "hard-surface highway," the number of flats you would have to fix along the way, or the countless times the radiator would boil over.

But by golly, (and this is the second point), when you got somewhere (like Ozark) it was an adventure. It was a different place, and you looked around, and explored, and got acquainted with those good "jovial, sociable, and appreciable" hill folks. You looked at the buildings and the houses, ate in the restaurants, shopped in the stores, learned about its history, and, in general, had a humming good time.

Today, most of us know the smaller towns around White River country only because we see their signs as we zip by them on our way somewhere else. And that's a shame, because in most of them, if we would only take time, we could discover many new pleasures and treasures.

Ozark for instance.

The Finley River still runs through Ozark, although the Frisco hasn't for some time. The court house presides over a busy county seat square with streets so wide, traffic runs both ways around it. The Appetite Cafe is gone, but the Back Porch Cafe and a variety of other eating places serve the hungry traveler. Some folks come to Ozark for the antique stores and gift shops, while others visit rodeos and bull rides, county fairs, crafts festivals—and, of course, murder trials in the courthouse.

"I don't like to go to town to buy something new,

if I can find something old that I like

better. It just makes sense."

The Wayne Holmes Home

Its not unusual in the Ozarks to find houses that seem to have been put together from materials scavenged from the aftermath of a tornado. You know the type—two or three different kinds of siding, some sheets of corrugated tin, roof shingles of various hues, front porch propped up with combinations of concrete block, hedge poles, and flat rock, the stove pipe of a wood-burning stove poking out through the wall.

Often we don't admire these cobbled-together houses. We feel sorry for the owners and hope they will soon be able to go to the lumber yard and replace all those old, used parts with brand new ones. But for some people, salvage is a matter of choice, not necessity. Wayne Holmes is a prime example.

I don't like to go to town and buy something new, if I can find
something old that I like better. It just makes sense.

Wayne and Mary Lou Holmes have recently settled into their new home—actually its the second home that they have built making extensive use of materials salvaged from other buildings.

Our previous house, for example, I believe had, I counted one time,
materials from 87 different sites in that house, including materials
from six or seven barns. There's lots and lots of barns that are being
torn down—have been torn down and are being torn down—that
have wonderful pine or oak timbers or wood that to me are
aesthetically pleasing.

The home of Wayne and Mary Lou Holmes is nothing like the clarty hodgepodge I described at the beginning. It is well designed, warm, and comfortable, and looks like it belongs exactly where it sits, in its sheltered site above Flat Creek, not far from the Barry County hamlet of McDowell.

There's much to admire in this handsome house, especially the attractive wood floor on the main level. The floorboards are random sizes, some as wide as 12 to 14 inches, and they're a full inch thick. How did they come by these beautiful boards?

> *I'm kind of scanning the roadway, roadside, as we drive around various places, looking for materials, and I spotted an old schoolhouse that had obviously been vacant for probably 20 years— had a lot of flagstone on it. Though of course, flagstone's not in vogue, I find that I like it I like it a lot. And I found out who owned it and offered him $500 for the building, which he was glad to get. But after my grandson and I took the rock off, or were taking it off, we saw the boxing, both inside and out, was red oak, and when you first took the rocks off it was as red as that is [indicating a chair cover]. Course, as the sun was on it, then it turned gray. I was a little dubious about it, frankly, but Mary Lou, who served as a general contractor for the building of the house, she was pretty adamant about wanting this for the floor, and I said, "Well, let's do it," and we had an accommodating and obliging carpenter who put them down, and then we had them sanded.*

Wayne's interest in home building goes back to stories he heard about his great-grandfather's rock house in northern Kansas. His dad was not in good health, but, as Wayne says, "Sometimes he wasn't of a mind to work, even when he could."

> *There were six of us—six kids. He and my mother were not temperamentally suited—she was a terrifically hard working person. But, about every two years we moved. We rented, or sharecropped, and the houses were inadequate. I'm sure as he thought about what had gone awry financially, that he often was nostalgic about the old stone house in northern Kansas. A lot of the stories he told, although they weren't exactly about the house itself, it seemed to me had to do with the stone house nevertheless.*

The fabled rock house of a great-grandfather he had never known stuck in the mind of the boy. How wonderful it would be to have such a home.

As I grew older and was able to afford building a house, it seemed to me to make sense economically, and aesthetically, to use materials at hand. And there's lots and lots of rocks and there's lots and lots of timbers. It's a combination of things, I think, that has led me to where I'm taking slate off a building, slate that was going to be taken to the dump. Or rock that's going to be used as fill. Or timbers that came from an old Joplin railroad station. Pine timbers that were 36 feet long and 4 x 12's that could be bought relatively at a bargain.

Wayne did not salvage an old King heater to heat the house. A high-efficiency Swedish wood- burning stove has that job. But there's lots of rock—about 175 tons of it, Wayne estimates, and lots of Ozarks lumber in this friendly and liveable house.

It should be liveable. It's had lots of experience.

PEOPLE

She began her "memory story" when she was 83

years old. It is a remarkable piece of writing by a

sensitive and observant writer, and provides a

first-hand account of life in the early Ozarks.

Aunt Margaret

All of us, I suppose, have our favorite aunts. I remember one in particular from my childhood. She was a warm and indulgent and fussy type who spoiled me shamelessly when I traveled by train to see her in Kansas City—that big, thrilling, mysterious city, so far away from my Ozarks home. She saved stacks of funny papers for me to read, and she delighted in stuffing me with hamburgers and french fries and ice cream and other delicacies while we toured the wonders of Swope Park.

I'll never forget my Kansas City aunt. She provided me with some precious childhood memories, and gave an Ozarks farm boy a glimpse of a bigger, exciting world. But it is another aunt, Aunt Margaret, who fills my thoughts today.

I have heard my mother say that when she and father went to housekeeping they moved into an unfinished log cabin, on a dirt floor and built a fire in the wash kettle, until father could make a fireplace and build a stick chimney and daub it with mud.

The voice is that of Minrose Quinn, a friend and colleague, but the words are those of my great aunt, Margaret Gilmore Kelso, my grandfather's sister. She was born in 1855 and died 93 years later.

I must have met her when I was young, but to be quite truthful, I don't really remember her. Yet my image today of Aunt Margaret is as sharp and clear and warm as my memory of my Kansas City aunt. Because Aunt Margaret, in her later years, wrote a journal.

Often I have been asked to write a memory story of my life and have hesitated to do so because I have had so little schooling.

She began her "memory story" when she was 83 years old. It is a remarkable piece of writing by a sensitive and observant writer, and provides a first-hand account of life in the early Ozarks.

Aunt Margaret's ancestors, and mine, came to the Ozarks in the early 1830s:

> *I have heard my father say that my grandfather made five trips from Tennessee to this country on horseback, all alone through the wilderness, to spy out the land. On the fifth trip he split rails and built a pen around the spring to hold down his claim, then went back to Tennessee and brought his family. Several families came here with him at that time, all in oxdrawn wagons. They were six weeks on the way.*

She describes a childhood life that was, in many ways, a frontier existence. They had no matches. If the fire happened to go out, they had to go to the neighbors to get more. "Borrowing fire" it was called.

> *I remember one morning when Mother got up the fire was out. She awakened me and I started on the run to borrow fire. I went to Uncle George Thomas's place. On the way the wild turkeys were coming off the roost and running out onto the road ahead of me. They kept to the road until they had to cross a little branch, and there they scattered. Wild turkeys were so plentiful. I know now there must have been seventy-five or a hundred in the bunch, maybe more. I went on to Mr. Thomas's place, got my fire between two long pieces of bark and ran all the way home. When I reached home, Mother was standing at the door waiting for the fire, and soon had breakfast ready.*

The Battle of Wilson's Creek has been exhaustively written about in terms of military strategy, troop movements, Bloody Hill, the death of General Lyons. Six year old Margaret only knew that her mother was so worried she didn't fix the children anything to eat all day.

> *My mother walked the floor all day, and wrung her hands and cried until the noise of the big guns ceased. It must have been five o'clock in the evening before she got us anything to eat. We children were too young to understand, and followed her around and begged her to tell us why she cried. She would place her hands on our heads and say, "Oh, children! Oh, children!" My brother and I would lay our heads on the ground, and we could hear the guns and feel the earth tremble.*

Toward the end of her journal she reflected on her long life, and marveled at the progress she had seen in her lifetime:

> *It is a far cry from the ox team to the automobile and the flying*
> *machine; from the Indian trails to the paved highway; from the log*
> *schoolhouse to the well-equipped consolidated school.*
> *The improvement over the old ways is so great. I certainly am not*
> *among those who are crying for "the good old days." I have had*
> *more comfort in my latter days than I ever had before. I do not yearn*
> *for the inconveniences of past years.*

Aunt Margaret didn't really want to write her "memory story." "I have so little schooling," she said. "It will have many mistakes in spelling, phrasing and punctuation." Perhaps someday I'll quit reading her journal for the history, the heritage, and the love that pour from every page, and correct it for grammar.

Perhaps. But I doubt it.

In today's Ozarks there is an amazing variety of ways of making a living. With some exceptions—deep sea fishing, for example, or beach volley-ball—it's difficult to imagine an occupation that isn't represented in the Ozarks.

Suzann Ledbetter

U sed to be, when you came across somebody you didn't know very well, one of the first questions that worked its way into the conversation was, "What do you do for a living?" To know people, you had to know about them— where they lived, who their family was, and how they made their livelihood.

Early on, people made a living in the Ozarks primarily from the land itself— fishing, trapping and hunting, later farming and timbering. As the population increased and communities grew, so did the need for individuals providing more specialized services—milling, black smithing, store keeping, school teaching, doctoring, lawyering, and the like.

In today's Ozarks there is an amazing variety of ways of making a living. With some exceptions—deep sea fishing, for example, or beach volleyball—it's difficult to imagine an occupation that isn't represented in the Ozarks.

*I'm a writer. I'm not an author. Grisham is an author. You've got to
make a lot of money to call yourself that. I'm also kind of diversified.
I do a humor column for Family Circle magazine. I'm doing novels,
and Random House has graciously put together some of my Family
Circle columns into a hard bound book.*

Writer, author, whatever—the fact is that Suzann Ledbetter is working full time out of her Nixa, Missouri home, putting words on paper, and being paid for it. "I've been a writer all my life," she says, "but I just started getting money for it about 10 years ago."

*I've always written. What it amounts to, as I tell people, is that I now
get paid for what I used to get grounded for. Which is a smart mouth
and making things up [laughs].*

Suzann is one of a large, and apparently increasing, number of people who live in the Ozarks, and who make their living in a most difficult profession, writing. Why are there so many writers here?

Mostly because it's a cheap place to live, and it's a nice place to live, and you can be as isolated as you want to be and as social as you want to be.

Organizations like the Ozarks Writer's League, or OWL, of which Suzann is President, provide support for writers.

And you have contacts—you don't have to live in New York to write, if you have the contacts there. And thanks to fax machines and stuff like that, it's becoming less important to really live in the publishing centers.

Being a writer involves more than sitting at home before the word processor. When I spoke with Suzann, she had just heard that her publisher had scheduled her for a 10-city tour to promote her newest book, *Trinity Strike.* This would not be her first experience with touring:

I've done two tours with Random House, the first one on The Toast Always Lands Jelly Side Down, *and ended up on the* Today Show, *which was the scariest thing I've ever done in my whole life. And the second book,* I Have Everything I Had Twenty Years Ago, Except Now It's All Lower, *was done in May. And you just travel around and do TV and radio and go to book stores. It's fun. It's exhausting, but it's fun.*

Suzann says she is still amazed that she can string a few sentences together, and when she reads them back, they sound OK. They apparently sound OK to other people as well. Two years ago she received the Spur Award for Short Non-Fiction from the Western Writers of America for her biography, *Nellie Cashman, Prospector and Trailblazer.*

That was a major honor. I didn't even know Western Writers of America existed until a bunch of us from the Ozarks went to Jackson, Wyoming to see Jory Sherman receive his. And be darned if two years later Jory Sherman wasn't seated at the table, watching me receive mine, and Texas Western Press, for the Nellie Cashman Biography.

Jory Sherman is an Ozarks writer who lives at Branson, and has more than 150 books to his credit.

Suzann's latest book is a novel, *Trinity Strike,* and is based on the life of Nellie Cashman. There are movie options on both the novel and the biography, but Suzann isn't planning her Oscar acceptance speech yet.

You might as well go to Quik Trip and buy a lottery ticket because a lot of things get optioned but very few get made.

Suzann has a message for parents—encourage your kids to write.

Pay attention to your kid's stories. And have them tell them, and don't interrupt 'em, and if they're in written form, don't fix the commas. It's the idea that counts.

If Suzann has her way, more and more Ozarkers will be answering the question, "What do you do for a living?" with the proud answer, "I'm a writer!"

"In a little while others were induced to dance

and from this others took it up until nearly every

one present — men, women, boys and girls —

joined in a general dance."

Silas Turnbo

"I am nothing but a poor scribbler." was the way Silas Turnbo once described himself.

This poor scribbler was a pioneer collector of Ozarks folklore and history who amassed one of the most important collections of Ozarks material ever assembled.

A portion of this vast collection has recently been published by the University of Arkansas Press as *The White River Chronicles of S. C. Turnbo: Man and Wildlife on the Ozarks Frontier.*

Lynn Morrow is one of the editors of the book. He is a Missouri historian and Director of Local Records for the Missouri State Archives.

> *Silas Claiborne Turnbo was born in a log cabin on Beaver Creek,*
> *Taney County, Missouri, on May 26, 1844. Although it was then a*
> *sparsely settled wilderness, the land around him already was*
> *undergoing great changes from that found by the very first white men*
> *to penetrate the upper White River region.*

Jim Keefe is a wildlife biologist and is retired from the Missouri Department of Conservation. He is the other editor.

> *These first-wave immigrants found bottom lands covered with cane*
> *and open forests with occasional tracts of pine trees, interspersed*
> *with broad prairies.*
> *There were bear, buffalo, elk, deer, panther, and wolves without*
> *number. These were what the first families sought, for food and for*
> *hides, to clothe themselves with, and to sell to traders for the few*
> *necessities the land would not provide.*

Most of Turnbo's stories come from the Arkansas and Missouri counties whose drainage flows into the White River. The Turnbo collection is among the earliest assembled writings about the antebellum Ozarks, and surely it must be the largest.

Many of Turnbo's stories are about wildlife. One, entitled "A hungry bear eats his last mess of pork," was told to Turnbo by a widow lady who lived in Marion County, Arkansas. Jim Keefe reads a portion of the story:

> [My husband] Joe cleared and fenced enough ground in three years to raise plenty to live on, the soil was so fertile that it produced big ears of corn and monster pumpkins.
>
> In the fall of 1830, Joe enclosed three acres of ground adjoining the yard fence with heavy poles and rails and put three of our best hogs in there to make bacon of them. They were fed on corn and pumpkins until they were exceedingly fat and were ready to be butchered.
>
> One morning early, Joe went to the lot and found that a bear had entered the enclosure and killed the hog and had carried it to the fence and, after pushing off some of the top rails, threw the hog over the fence and climbed over and picked up the hog again and passed on through the cane and up the face of the bluff on the east side of the hollow opposite the house. I do not know how it happened that we never heard the bear kill the hog nor the dogs never found it out.

Lynn Morrow reads from a story about a man living on Little North Fork in Ozark County, Missouri, who had been invited to a big log rolling.

> There was a big crowd there with plenty of whisky and hard work to do. But we got all the logs piled by night. At night, just before supper time, Sam Bevins, who was an excellent violinist, tuned up his fiddle and began playing on it.
>
> At this Mac Holmes and his daughter Sarah stepped onto the middle of the floor and commenced to dance. This was a great surprise to us for Mac and his daughter were members of the Freewill Baptist Church. In a little while others were induced to dance and from this others took it up until nearly every one present—men, women, boys and girls—joined in a general dance. I forgot I had a wife who I

ought to have known was waiting for me at home. It was the awfullest
dance I ever attended. Part of us got dog drunk and the remainder of
the men and boys were not far behind this.

On the following morning I come to my senses and, oh, how mean I
felt for not returning back home as I had promised my wife. Some of
the men proposed to take Mr. Holmes and his daughter down to the
creek and rebaptize them for we blamed them with it. They were
members of the church and they ought to have set us a better example
than to be leaders in a dance. We all said that they had not been
baptized deep enough in the water. But we did not take them.

In 1913 an impoverished and ailing Silas Turnbo wrote to a Kansas historian,
W. W. Connelly, offering to sell his massive manuscript for any "reasonable
price." A few weeks later Connelly sent Turnbo a money order for $27.50. "I
could not deny an old friend in need," he wrote Turnbo, "so I made extra effort
and got the money."

How pleased and proud Turnbo would be with this fine publication of a part
of his works.

"Who sympathized with you when your little girl

was sick? Was it your home merchant, or was it

Sears and Roebuck? Who carried you last winter

when you were out of a job and had no money?

Was it Montgomery Ward and Co. Or

was it your home merchant?"

Newspapers I

Editors

In 1931, Mr. Charles U. Becker, who was then Missouri's Secretary of State, delivered a speech to a meeting of journalists in Indianapolis. Becker, who was a former newspaperman himself, introduced his topic by saying,

> Ladies and gentlemen, with your gracious permission, I shall discuss
> two kinds of newspapers—the metropolitan press, which is a most
> serious menace to society, religion, business, and good government,
> and the country press, to which the people must turn for truth and the
> saving of our political parties, without which no republican govern-
> ment can endure.

Now while Mr. Becker may have had his tongue firmly planted in his cheek, there is much truth in his praise of the "country press," or what you and I would probably call "weeklies."

A long time friend, Dale Freeman, shares my love of old newspapers. Dale started newspapering in his home town of Mansfield, in Wright County, Missouri, when he was about 14 years old and was Editor of Springfield Newspapers for many years.

> I used to tell the Ozarks Editors Association, when they had such a
> group (I'm not sure they do have now), I said, "Hey, you're the guys
> that are at the forefront and I can't tell you how much I appreciate
> you, because a small town editor, number one, a good one, he had to
> be the most courageous editor of all."

It took courage, after all, to go have coffee at the local cafe with the guy you had lambasted in print just the day before. Or to face in church on Sunday the members of the Ladies Group after your paper printed the wrong date in the notice about the sociable to raise money for the missionary to China.

The editor's personality and stamp of individuality would be found in every issue. Through the columns of his paper the editor sought to bring his readers, and the whole community, into modern times.

Most editors were proud of their communities. The editor of the *Ash Grove Commonwealth,* in Greene County, could hardly contain his pride at the success of Ash Grove's Fall street fair in 1905. Dale Freeman is the editor's voice:

> *Taken all in all, our fair was the biggest thing that ever happened in this part of the United States. It is conceded by all present that Ash Grove is at the exact center of the cosmos. The hub around which all created suns and worlds revolve.*

Such bragging came as no surprise to the readers of the *Commonwealth.* After all, that paper for years carried on its masthead the modest slogan, "Official Organ of the World."

Editors were quick to use their papers to point out problems they saw in the community.. Editors harangued their readers about the deterioration of the streets and sidewalks, animals running loose in the streets or buying from mail order catalogues rather than from local merchants.

"Who sympathized with you when your little girl was sick,"one editor scolded. "Was it your home merchant, or was it Sears and Roebuck? Who carried you last winter when you were out of a job and had no money? Was it Montgomery Ward and Co. or was it your home merchant?"

Some editors avoided politics in their papers completely, but others were strongly biased in their political leanings. Editors liked to ridicule the opposition with mock prayers that they asserted were offered at rival political meetings. For example, an attack on the portly Grover Cleveland in 1894 entitled "Democratic Prayer," began

> *Thy neck, oh Cleveland, is like unto a male cow's neck, and thy head resembles a sickly turnip. The size of thy pants is enormous and thy lower bosom is beyond description. Thou art as graceful as a cow and as gentle as a hyena. The symmetry of thy person is like a mud fence after a rain storm.*

And so on in the same vein.

How mild, by comparison, is this more modern editor's good-humored analysis of a substantial Democratic defeat:

> *Some folks say the Democratic defeat was due to poor organization.*
> *Others say the organization is all right, but the party needs more zip*
> *and enthusiasm. Personally it looks to us like it needs two things, viz.,*
> *some rest and a damsite more votes.*

The editor's voice was important, but most subscribers were more interested in what was going on in their own communities.

> *Don Wilson and Oval Wilson made a trip to Springfield with fat hogs*
> *last Tuesday. They are planning to go again this Tuesday. Don is still*
> *reading "The People's Almanac." It's a very thick book.*

In the next White River Journal we'll take a closer look at how early newspapers gathered and reported local news.

Their copy included lots of names—who visited whom, who was sickly, who had sent a load of hogs to market. Names were the lifeblood of the newspaper industry.

Newspapers II

Country Correspondents

In the last Journal, I talked about early weekly newspapers. There were lots of them.

In 1904, the year of the great St. Louis World's Fair, there was an average of about six and a half weekly newspapers for every one of Missouri's 114 counties. And the Ozarks, both Arkansas and Missouri, had their share.

In the earlier Journal, I talked about how editors brought their own stamp of individuality and personality to their newspapers. My friend and former long-time Editor of Springfield Newspapers, Dale Freeman, who shares my passion for weeklies, read some good examples of editorial opinion. Here is another:

If we were forced to choose between Hades and Ozark County,
Missouri as our future destination, we would study long and loud before
making the choice for we figure the odds are rather in favor of Hades.

That was an editorial comment from the Salem, Arkansas Banner in 1895. The Gainesville, Missouri ball club, the Blues, was a real powerhouse, and had just whipped the Salem team by a score of 17 to 5. So the Arkansas editor was feeling a little tender. Naturally the Gainesville editor responded in his paper. The Salem man won't be required to worry about making a choice, he wrote, "A man who makes remarks like the above it seems to us is pretty well settled in favor of Hades in preference to any other place."

Although the editor's voice was important and colorful, most readers were more interested in what was going on in their own communities.

Local town news items were dropped off at the newspaper office, or picked up by the editor in his wanderings about town.

For news from surrounding rural communities, the editors depended upon volunteer country correspondents. Their copy included lots of names who visited whom, who was sickly, who had sent a load of hogs to market. Names were the lifeblood of the newspaper industry. Some examples:

T. R. Ray got caught in a corn shredder Tuesday. The cogs of the machine caught the seat of his pantaloons. The doctor took six stitches. Ron Murray and family Sundayed with home folks.

Monday while in town I saw Lon and Bess Hudson and Bess had a hand wrapped up. She had caught her thumb in the wringer washing machine and went to the doctor every other day for awhile.

Dale Freeman found this item in the Douglas County Herald:

Marvin Pare has been unlucky as far as being attacked by rabid animals. Last spring he was bitten by a cat that had rabies and this winter while cutting brush he was attacked by a rabid fox. Now he is taking more shots. This, on top of serving as Republican committeeman for the last few years, is more than any one man should have to go through with.

Some of these correspondents reported incidents with a colorful abandon and a disregard of libel laws that would make a modern editor blanch. For example, in writing about a successful protracted meeting, a correspondent reported:

There was quite a number of accessions from other churches besides those who heretofore joined and then danced themselves out of the church but came back to the fold. A few old toughs like Don Wilson, W. M. Randolph, H. W. Stewart, Alex West, Ab Stiffler and Mrs. Amos were all that made their escape, and they had to hide out.

Now that is aggressive evangelism!

Some correspondents went well beyond a listing of names. With the encouragement of their editors, they developed a journalistic style and a following among many faithful readers. Instead of a prosaic, "Well, winter's coming on," how about

Already the gypsy lass, October, is dancing our way on sandaled feet, tripping the brittle grass with gay abandon.

Whatever the style or the content, early newspapers would not have been the same without the country correspondents. Here is one of Dale Freeman's favorite items, and mine. It has everything—names, news, compassion, emotion.

Corbet Crain was over at Franks Saturday. Said he came by Orel Crain and asked Orel if he wanted to go along and he said Orel said he didn't feel good and he asked to take Orel to a doctor but he didn't want to go. And Corbet stopped by his daughters and told her to go over and see if he wanted to see a doctor. They went over and Orel was dead. Joyce came over to Franks and told Corbet. We all was upset. Everyone at Franks signed a get-well card. About 65 or 70 friends of Orel. We all was sorry that Orel didn't get the get well card in time.

"It's relaxing to come in from a hard day's work

and get in your buggy and take

a ride over the place."

Earl Maggard

Buggy Builder

About any way I drive from my home in southern Stone County, I see signs assuring me that if I need additional transportation, it is available. New and used car and truck lots are everywhere, and there are many places to buy boats, jet skis, ATV's, RV's, and tractors. It should not have surprised me, then, when my neighbor down the road put up a sign announcing that he had buggies for sale. And not only did he sell buggies, he made them as well.

I visited Earl Maggard, buggy builder , at his home, shop, and sales office just south east of Reeds Spring Junction. I wondered where he learned the buggy trade:

> *I've known about buildin' buggies and wagons practically all my life.*
> *I was raised over by Forsyth. And then I got acquainted with the*
> *Amish people. And they showed me all the fine points to makin' bug-*
> *gies. So they really helped me out and I think they're fine folks. But I*
> *got my own shop now and, well, I added another storage building two*
> *weeks ago, so the buggy business is lookin' up.*

Where do your customers come from? I asked him. And why do people buy buggies, anyway?

> *I build buggies for everywhere. Oregon, California and Texas is a*
> *big buyer for the buggies. People that like parades, trail rides. Well,*
> *lot of 'em will buy a buggy and just set in front of their house cause*
> *it looks nice.*

Earl Maggard has been building buggies for 30 years. He was with the Shepherd of the Hills Farm for 25 years, not only building buggies as a tourist demonstration, but also occasionally acting as tour guide, and performing the role of Jim Lane in the Shepherd of the Hills Pageant. Recently he decided he'd rather work for himself, on his own schedule. And that schedule has kept him busy.

Earl says he likes to keep a few buggies ahead if he can, but when I was there his inventory was down to only three, a small buckboard, a surrey, and a doctor buggy—a one seater. I wondered about his competition, and if they are all doing as well as he is:

I have no idea. There's some builders... but a lot of times the price is so high. I found that out. Now I build a small buckboard. I've sold many of them, and I see—I'm not calling any names or telling where— but the same buggy that I sell for $1400, a buckboard, they get $2995. I don't know whether they sell any or not. I'd rather have the price lower and sell more buggies. Keep me busy, keep me out of trouble.

The small buckboard he referred to is only about 3/4 the size of a full-sized buckboard. The first one he made was on special order for a fellow who wanted to hitch his llama to it. The little buckboard came out so well that Earl kept on making them, although more of them are probably pulled by ponies than by llamas.

What do you have to know to be a buggy maker? I asked him. He was stumped for a minute.

Well, I don't know hardly how to answer that, but you've gotta know how to put the wheels together, that is one of the main things. You can't turn one spoke this way and the other one the other way. If you do, you'll have a crooked wheel. So there's a lot of things to do. The old timers figured that out. I guess it was kind of handed down to me from way back.

Earl bends his buggy wheels from hickory, shapes and forms the spokes, and finishes them with a hard rubber tire. The bearings in the hub are quite different now than they were years ago. In the old days, they were metal to metal. Earl told of asking an old timer how far it was to a certain place, and being told, "Oh, about three axle greases away."

Now, they have bearings like a car, so that makes them pull real easy, and you put that hard rubber tire on there and it don't go down the road a-rattlin'.

Well, I've about decided I'd rather have a buggy than a jet ski. Especially after Earl told his last story:

> *Now, I bought a ranch over by Ava, here, probably 30 years ago. And the first thing I did when I bought the ranch, I built me a buggy—a doctor buggy. It's relaxing to come in from a hard day's work and get in your buggy and take a ride over the place.*

And lots quieter than a jet ski, too.

"I've seen 'em stand and chew up dry leaves and

they weren't that desperate for anything to eat.

You know, they were standing in green grass

chewing on an old sycamore leaf."

Raising Buffalo

Not too long ago, I went out one Saturday morning with a friend of mine to feed his livestock. He's renting some pasture out east of Branson where he keeps his six heifers and a bull. I was interested in seeing them because these particular animals happen to be buffalo—a species of livestock unique in Taney County.

Darrell Testerman has been a conservation agent for 33 years—23 of those in Taney County. I helped him unload several bags of cattle feed from his pickup, and then stood by while he scattered a couple of buckets full in the feeding trough. The animals all trotted up and started eating, snorting, pushing, shoving and poking each other with their short sturdy horns. They weren't particulary big. I asked how old they were:

> These are all young. These are all just last year's calves, so they're up
> close to a year and a half old now. They're longer-lived than cattle,
> they live longer, and they get started a little slower, so actually these
> calves won't be breeding age, the heifers or the bull, until next year.
> They'll breed at two and then not calve until they're three years old.

Darrell introduced me to "the girls," and their friend, Cody. Besides Laverne and Shirley, I met Dee Dee, Peggy, Kathy, and Janet. Aren't those the names of the Lennon Sisters, from the Lawrence Welk show? Darrell just grinned.

How big will the girls get, I wondered?

> Well, they'll almost double in size, from what they are now. An aver
> age cow will weight a thousand pounds, up to 12 hundred, and the
> bull that you see out there is about a 700 pounder, and he may get as
> big as a ton.

I also wondered how raising buffalo compared with raising, say, beef cattle?
Well, the one thing that really scares you when you read all the books, is the fencing that's required, because they still have a lot of wild instinct to 'em. You feed 'em every day, and they stand around, they look pretty tame, they walk right by us here, you think, "Well, they're just a cow with a little hump on their back.

As they get older and heavier, Darrell said, these animals will turn into "fur-covered bulldozers:"
And they'd really go through these normal cattle panels that'll hold about any beef cattle. So, at this size you can handle them in regular facilities and it isn't a problem, but two years from now, I'm going to have to have heavier corrals, when I get ready to put these up.

I was surprised to learn that buffalo don't take as much food as beef cattle:
They definitely eat less than cattle. I don't know how much, but many of the figures show they eat like a third what cattle do out on the range. They'll eat a poorer quality of grass, and some of the weeds that cattle won't eat. I've seen 'em stand and chew up dry leaves and they weren't that desperate for anything to eat. You know, they were standing in green grass chewing on an old sycamore leaf.

I've never eaten buffalo meat. Does it taste like beef?
A lot of people think that buffalo meat may be just a little sweeter, but it's definitely as good as the best beef you've ever had. But, as I say, if you set down to a burger or a good steak, either one, and no one told you, you'd say, "Boy, that's a great piece of steak," but you probably wouldn't notice the difference in taste.

Something that tastes that good must be bad for you, right? Not so, says Darrel, buffalo meat is very nutritious. The cholesterol rating is lower than skinless chicken, there is 35% more protein than in beef, and it has very little fat.

You can't normally find buffalo meat stocked at your local supermarket, so it needs to be ordered by mail. And it gets pretty pricey. One catalogue I looked at listed buffalo tenderloins at $40 per pound. Buffalo burgers, more in my category anyway, could be had for only about $11 a pound.

Why is buffalo meat so expensive? Right now, the demand for buffalo meat far outweighs the supply—a situation Darrell hopes to help correct as his herd grows and he starts marketing his animals.

In the early days, I learned, buffalo ranged all over North America, from Florida to Canada. Canada has a woods buffalo, Darrell told me, which is a little different from the plains buffalo:

> And we've been saying 'buffalo' all the time, these are bison. It's a little hard for me to get the new word, but the actual true buffalo is the Asian, or the water buffalo. These are truly bison. Their technical name is Bison Bison, and so the American buffalo is a true bison.

Now I know that seven head of yearling buffalo, or bison, are not going to replace the large herds that ranged the Ozarks in early days, but its a good step backward. Good luck, Darrell!

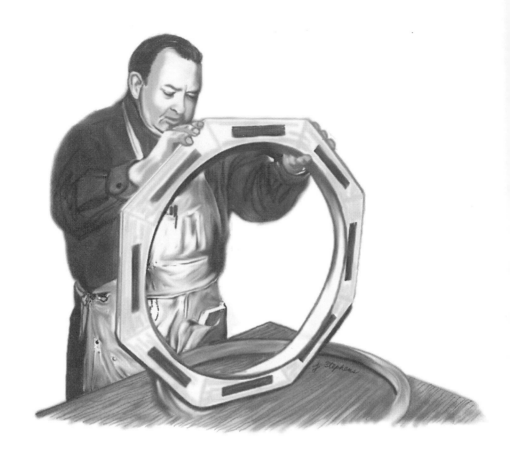

"When you work by yourself, you don't clean up

too often. You climb over everything till you can't

stand it, then you'll take a day out

or two and clean up."

Gene Turney

Wood Worker

A year or so ago, my wife saw an ad for quilting hoops in the Ozarks Mountaineer. "I need one," she said, "let's go look at them. I probably won't buy," she said, "but let's at least look."

That's how we became acquainted with The Quilting Bee, Gene Turney's wood shop in Omaha, Arkansas. About a month ago, we went back to Omaha to talk to Mr. Turney about being a woodworker in the Ozarks.

You know, it's difficult to make a living in the Ozarks, and I do what I do. I mean, I've done woodwork all my life and I love it. So any kind of woodwork that I haven't tried, well, I won't say no to it.

Looking around Gene Turney's small shop on highway 65, it's difficult to believe that there's much in the way of woodworking he hasn't tried. He points out a few of his creations:

You know, there's some columns over there and nobody necessarily makes columns. That picture on the wall, staircases, not too many people do a circular staircase, things of that kind. This is an antique reproduction here on that cradle, and so is the chest over there. I just like to do interesting work. I made this table in 1952, just to see if I could, you know, The cabriolet legs are interesting and it has a leather top. I tooled that. I decided that wasn't my long suit either. But it's a pretty little table.

It is. And so are the quilting hoops that have become his speciality. Gene began specializing in quilting hoops after having a heart attack and triple bypass surgery. His doctor told him to do some lighter work than the columns, cabinets, and staircases he had been building. He teamed up with a friend, Mel Pollack, who has a shop in Harrison. I wondered if they build all their own components for their hoops?

> *Yup. Mel makes the bases on the stands for the hoops and I make the hoops here and we work together on it but since I'm on the highway, we display it here.*

Gene says he has always been interested in woodworking, ever since he took high school shop when he was about 13. Then he received invaluable training when he went to wood pattern maker's school in the Navy.

> *They have repair ships in the Navy and you go from this school to the repair ship and you do pattern work right on board these ships. They have a foundry and everything. They do it all. You can bring a ship alongside for repairs and they can build anything they need right there from scratch. I mean they make the patterns, they make the castings, you machine it, put a part back in quicker than you can order it from stateside.*

I wandered around Gene's shop with him. It is crammed full of machinery, but nothing very esoteric—saws, routers, sanders, drills—about what you'd find in any home shop, only more of them.

> *I've got probably twenty-two small machines out there and a lot of portable equipment, and once I get set up on something I pretty well just go on one machine to the next. When you work by yourself, you don't clean up too often. You climb over everything till you can't stand it, then you'll take a day out or two and clean up.*

Their marketing consists mainly of going to quilting shows, and by word of mouth. But that pays off.

> *We haul everything we can put in the van and even take a trailer once in a while. This year we'll probably only do four shows. You've got to come home and build it too. There's nobody here and so it's complicated. We had two shows in October and that was very difficult because if you sell everything at one show you've got to make something real quick for the next one. And so, we got caught and we won't do that again.*

Gene laminates his own hardwood and bends the hoops himself. He works mostly in oak, but also offers walnut and cherry. Some people, he says, buy the hoops mostly to decorate with. And I understand why. Martha, of course, on our first "let's just go look" trip to the Quilting Bee, came away bearing a beautifully finished 29 inch oak hoop. I admire the craftsmanship, the texture of the wood, and especially the big wooden screw knob that clamps the two pieces of the hoop together. Martha says its comfortable to use and holds the quilt in place well. I think it's too good looking a piece of wood craft to be covered up by a quilt. Martha disagrees. Martha is winning.

And the quilt is almost done.

There's not an endless supply of water down

there, Lefty says. He's seen the water table drop

in the southern end of the country well over a

hundred feet in the last ten years.

Water

Lefty Evens

Seems like about every where you drive in the Ozarks you see water wells being drilled. New homes, new golf courses, new condos, new trailer parks. I got to wondering about our underground water supply and the whole business of well drilling.

Lefty Evans, of Crane, in Stone County, Missouri, has been drilling wells for over 30 years. I asked him how well drilling technology has changed in that time:

> *[Laughter] I guess my first drill rig that I purchased was a used machine, and I think, brand new it was around $70,000. And I could expect, on a good day with that, to average around 200 feet a day. I purchased two new machines in the past three years, that they were well over $400,000 apiece, and I can expect out of each one of these machines, I can expect five to six hundred feet a day. So, that's really speeded things up for us, you know.*

I was pretty sure that Lefty didn't wander around with a forked willow branch to find water. But I did wonder how he knew just where to locate his drilling rig:

> *The safest place to assume to drill a well is on the high side of your property, and on the levelest part of it you can find, as a rule the most stable part of the ground. When you just stand and look at it, you know. You take old well drillers, they can pretty well just look at the ground and know about what to expect, and a lot of times it usually plays out just by observing, you know.*

I wondered, also, how deep the average residential well was. About 600 feet, Lefty told me. That gets down to his main source of water, the Jefferson formation.

And then we'll encounter Roubidoux. In Stone County here, you can
figure Roubidoux formation pretty simply. It's usually 500 feet above
sea level. For example, if you're 1200 feet above sea level, it'll be 700
feet to the top of Roubidoux.

There's not an endless supply of water down there, Lefty says. He's seen the
water drop in the southern end of the county well over a hundred feet in the past
ten years.

We just keep going deeper and deeper all the time. As a matter of fact,
I've probably redrilled eight or ten wells in the past year that I had
drilled in the late 60s and early 70s that have gone dry in the southern
end of the county. And a lot of people think, you know, Roubidoux for-
mation has a lot of water in it. But Missouri Geological Survey will tell
you, you know, you can expect from 30 to 50 gallons of water a minute
out of Roubidoux formation. But I can show you some areas now that
I've drilled into Roubidoux and it's more like 10 or 15 gallons.

Does this mean we're running out of water in our underground water table?
No one can really tell us about our water supply, because we're really
not certain just how much is there. I don't have any idea nor does
anyone else that I know, how much is there, as I say, and how long it's
going to last, but the demand is going to have to be eased up because
one thing is certain—we can't continue the way we're going and
maintain a pure water supply for everyone.

The average household uses about 300 gallons of water per day, Lefty says,
not including watering lawns, gardens, and that type of thing. A motel, though,
might use 10-15 thousand gallons of water a day or more. And cities, like
Kimberling City and Branson, use several million gallons a day. If that's all
drawn from our underground aquifers, Lefty worries, it's not being replenished
nearly as fast as we're taking it out.

But, to me, it looks like it's going to come to the point that the cities,
such as Branson and Kimberling City and our major cities in Stone
Country are going to have to go to alternate water supplies—either
go to Table Rock Lake or Taneycomo, or whatever.

Several years ago, Lefty, along with seven other drillers from around the state, was asked to put together some regulations concerning the drilling industry. Most of these recommendations were adopted by the state legislature and are now law. They're good laws, Lefty says, not only for the consumer, but for his industry as well.

You have to have two year's experience before you can drill a well. Anybody can't just go out there… there's a lot of difference in a water well and pokin' a hole in the ground. And there are some standards that you need to follow, some procedures you need to do. I've seen that really improve in the last few years.

Drillers must certify that each well has been drilled to state specifications. These specifications include not drilling within a hundred feet of a septic tank or a sewer line. A well must be set back 10 feet from property lines and 25 feet from power lines. A private well must be cased a minimum of 80 feet, or 30 feet into solid bedrock, whichever occurs first. The driller is liable for the casing for three years after construction.

These strict standards help protect our wells from pollution, but Lefty keeps returning to his theme of concern—the problem of the enormous amount of water that is being taken from our underground sources.

I think it's a problem that we need to address real quickly, because it's closer to being a serious problem than most people want to realize.

EVENTS

"As I was watching this man, a screeching,

wavering yell from the other end almost boosted

me out of the boat. It roared and soared and

echoed back and forth between the hills

until it finally died out entirely."

A Fishing Trip to the Buffalo River

A short story written by my good friend L. B. Cook, down at Theodosia, came into my hands the other day. L. B. claims it's true. At least as true as memories from the 1930s will allow. But what does it matter, anyhow? It's a good story.

He called his yarn, "A yell of a fishing trip." I didn't much care for the title, until I read his tale. Then it made sense. I asked L.B. to read you parts of his story:

This happened entirely too many years back to remember all facts in
the proper perspective, but I still have some wonderful memories.

It seems that L. B. and two of his young Joplin buddies decided to take a fishing trip down on the Buffalo River, in northwest Arkansas.

We had to haul enough food and gear to last us the week we wanted
to stay. We finally settled on a spot at the mouth of Cedar Creek, a
few miles downstream from the small community of Rush.

They made it to Rush on a Sunday morning, and were directed by some natives down to a small schoolhouse, where, the boys were told, they might be able to find somebody to rent them a boat.

We made it fine and arrived at this old schoolhouse, the one room
kind, just before noon. We learned that the building was used for
school on weekdays, and on Sundays it served as a church.

The owner of the john boat the boys had seen tied just below the school house was still in church, but he soon came out.

We told him who we were and that we hoped to camp out there for
about a week to fish, and we wanted to rent his boat from him to use
for trotlining. Without blinking an eye, he told us he wouldn't think of

renting us his boat.

*I guess we looked pretty disappointed, because he came right back
and added that he didn't say we couldn't use his boat he just said he
wouldn't rent it.*

He did ask one favor of the boys. If the river came up to where his kids
couldn't wade across the shoals to get to and from school, would the boys mind
"settin' 'em across?" Needless to say, the boys agreed.

*As we headed back towards camp that first noon we noticed a long,
lanky young fellow, about our own age, standing off to one side of the
camp. We invited him to come into camp and have some lunch and
coffee with us.*

They learned his name was Paul Beavers, and his folks lived "just over the
mountain," in Rea Valley, on White River. Paul was invited to join the Joplin
boys for the remainder of their fishing trip.

*Later in the week our trotline quit producing as good as it had been
so we decided to move it to another hole, just below camp. That
involved running the shoals with the boat. Paul said that he and I
could do that with no trouble at all. I wasn't too sure. The riffle was
deep and swift, and full of room-sized rocks here and there that could
easily change your location from inside the boat to outside, and fast.*

They made it down below where the shoals curled into deeper blue water, and
were stringing the trot line:

*I happened to look downstream and saw the figure of a man walking
in a field up on about the second bench. The field was a good three-
quarters of a mile from us.*

*As I was watching this man, a screeching, wavering yell from the other
end almost boosted me out of the boat. It roared and soared and echoed
back and forth between the hills until it finally died out entirely.*

*Before I could even begin to figure out why Paul had let out that awful
howl, another entirely different yell came rolling back upstream to us
from this other party. And then he was completely out of our sight.*

*Paul picked up the long boat pole and asked me what I would think of
a mess of roasting ears for supper that evening. Then he said we just*

might find a ripe watermelon to go with that corn.

Paul then poled the boat downstream, towards where they had seen the visitor and pulled up on the gravel.

He said we'd go pick some corn. Then I began to balk a little. I knew
we were going to get into a lot of trouble if we got into someone's
cornfield and watermelon patch without them knowing about it.

The two young men picked some choice roasting ears, and selected two ripe watermelons.

By then I was sure that when we headed back towards the boat with
that corn and those melons there would sure be some buckshot follow-
ing close behind us.

Back in the boat, Paul explained what had been going on

He told me that all the natives in this country of steep hills and deep
hollers had their own particular yell. This was know by the others as a
means of identification. When he yelled at this man, whom he assumed
was the owner of the field, that told him who Paul was and that he
would probably go into the field to pick a mess of corn, or whatever
else happened to be growing there. When the other man yelled back, it
told Paul that was the man he thought it was and that he knew who
Paul was, and it was alright for him to go on into the field.

Paul said that anytime this man got over into Rea Valley and wanted anything that grew there, it would be the same story in reverse.

The "arranged-for" roasting ears and watermelons ate plumb good
that night. Nothing beats fried fish and home-grown food at a time
like this, especially if it's prepared on an open fire in the beautiful
Buffalo River county. And with the gurgling river providing the dinner
music for us.

"It just killed the town. It was never rebuilt, and

the few people who did come back, or try to live

there, soon left, and the roads were blocked

up. It became private property."

The Melva Tornado

Hurricane Opal, which hit the Panhandle of Florida and the Gulf Barrier Islands in 1995, spread its devastation over a large area. Forecasters spotted the storm well out to sea, and warned people in advance. Nevertheless, there was still lots of damage, and some lives were lost.

While we may not have hurricanes in the Ozarks, we do have vicious tornados which often strike with little or no warning, and the ruin they cause can be complete. Like the tornado that wiped out the Taney County community of Melva in 1920.

Melva was a little town, I guess you could call it a town, on the railroad south of Hollister about three miles. It was on Turkey Creek, and it was built up on a ridge of a glade just east of the creek.

Ellen Massey of Lebanon has written a book on the life of Mary Elizabeth Mahnkey. At the time of the tornado, Mary Elizabeth and her husband Pres were living at Melva. Pres was running the general store and Mary Elizabeth was postmistress. I asked Ellen to tell me what she had learned about Melva, and about the storm. People had begun settling in the area as early as the 1880s, she said, for the mining—lead, copper, zinc.

And then in 1906, the White River Railroad came through there. It was a flag stop, and a lot of workers who were working on the railroad—not a lot, but there were two, maybe up to eight crews that would be living in Melva. There was a section house in the town for the foreman, there was a depot, which was a boxcar. But it had a ticket office and a storage place for freight and baggage.

Because of the railroad, Melva became important as a shipping center for fruits and vegetables.

> *There are a lot of orchards in the area—peach, apples, then there were strawberries and grapes, and tomatoes. And there was a canning factory there for tomatoes.*

There was a blacksmith shop, barber shop and a sawmill. Lots of lumber, ties, and cedar and oak posts went out on the railroad, as well as grain from the surrounding farms.

> *It had just one general store and a post office, but they had a hotel, which was two stories. And two sisters ran it—they were missionary women. They had a Sunday School and even a small library. There was a school there. In 1920 it had about 20 children.*

As the second decade of the 20th century began, the town was flourishing, and its future looked bright.

> *But on March the 11th, in 1920, a tornado came through. It was a very narrow tornado about 200 to 400 yards wide but it went right through Melva and it just wiped it out. The only thing left of the whole town after the tornado went through was the depot, the school house, and one house that Pres Mahnkey lived in.*
>
> *There were eight children killed, two pregnant women were injured badly, and later their babies died.*

The children weren't in school that day. Their teacher couldn't get across swollen, flooding Turkey Creek. Some of the boys were out walking along the creek, but they stayed well back from it. They were all afraid of water, for they couldn't swim.

When the boys finally noticed the storm, they ran to a neighbor's house, the house of Anna Box. Two Box families lived in this house.

> *So they all went into the house, this one house. And the house was picked up, turned upside down, and dumped into the swirling creek. And the children were small, and they were all swept down the creek except for one child, except for one Mahnkey boy. He was 12 and he managed to get hold of a tree and saved himself. The other children were swept down the creek and drowned. The two women that were in the house were big enough, heavy enough, that they weren't washed down.*

Seven of those who died were Box children, The eighth was seven-year old Bill Mahnkey. In her book, Ellen Massey writes, "It was the custom in the hills for neighbors to sit up with the dead. But that night, with so many in town dead, homeless, and injured, there was no one to come."

Melva doesn't exist anymore. The only way to get to where it used to be is through private land, or to walk down the railroad right-of-way, south out of Hollister.

It just killed the town. It was never rebuilt, and the few people who did come back, or try to live there, soon left, and the roads were blocked up, it became private property. The railroad quit stopping there, because there wasn't anything there, and the roads closed. In 1947, that was 27 years after the tornado, the map of the county didn't even mention Melba. So it had just completely disappeared.

The convening of the circuit court was the

occasion for the gathering of people from all over

the county, not only to conduct business with the

court, but to greet friends and neighbors

that you hadn't seen for a week."

Court Week

G reene County has recently acquired a new building in which to hold court. It's called a "Judicial Courts Facility," not a "courthouse." The Greene County Courthouse is still there, of course, but will no longer be used for trials. Instead, the Courthouse will now house only county offices, such as the Collector of Revenue, Planning and Zoning, and Business Regulation.

Now I'm glad Greene County has a better place to hold trials—one that is more comfortable and convenient for the jurors, and that has better security. At the same time, though, it's going to be a little strange to have a courthouse without any courts.

Early Ozarkers could not have imagined the courthouses in their county seat towns not having a courtroom. At least twice a year, once in the spring and again in the late fall, the small county seat towns of the Ozarks came alive with the excitement of court week. The convening of the circuit court was the occasion for the gathering of people from all over the county, not only to conduct business with the court, but to greet friends and neighbors and witness the drama of courtroom proceedings.

Juries were often selected from the men who happened to be on the streets at the time the sheriff was choosing a panel. Some families avoided going to town during the two months before court week for fear of being summoned for jury duty. Others, however, sought out jury duty and made themselves regularly available. One Texas County, Missouri, resident boasted to me that "from the time I became 21 years old, I don't suppose I missed a year of some court a-bein' on the jury, till they thought I got too old to know right from wrong."

The real-life drama of a courtroom trial held a fascination for Ozarkers, whether or not they had a special concern for the case. With almost equal interest they observed trials for burglary, peace disturbance, horse theft, divorce suits, and murder. The Barry County, Missouri man who beat his wife so violently that he wore out not only a buggy whip but a heavy limb from a peach tree as well, drew only a $20 fine on his guilty plea. The women from the surrounding community were not pleased. If they could have had their way, the *Cassville Republican* reported, "he would now be carrying a well-striped back himself."

Most trial lawyers of the day employed a flamboyant, emotional style of argument. At the murder trial of Hosea Bilyeu in Christian County, Missouri, the defense attorney, G. Purd Hayes, impersonated one of the murdered men. The local paper reported, "Hayes dressed himself in the clothing, trousers, shirt, and coat said to have been worn by Jimmy Bilyeu on the day of the massacre on which he gave up his life. Lawyer Hayes presented a striking spectacle, dressed in the bloody bullet-ridden clothing as he appeared before the jury in the garb of death. The spectators…held their breath in silence."

During court week, the hotels and boarding houses of the county seat town were soon crowded to capacity, and visitors who were unable to find lodging with acquaintances camped outdoors. Marvin Tong, who was a fine Ozarks historian and scholar, described how a judge accommodated a group of spectators during one cold winter term of court in Ozark County, Missouri. I've asked Dale Freeman to read Marvin's words:

> *They were having this murder trial and it'd come down along about two o'clock in the afternoon and it was time for the final argument before the jury with a couple of colorful lawyers. One of the natives in the back of the room raised his hand and asked if he could speak to the judge, which, you know, was kind of unusual, and the judge said yes, so this big fellow came up to him and told him, he says, "Now judge," he says, "it's going to be terribly cold tonight." He says, "It's turned bitter cold out there." He says, "You don't reckon you could put off them final arguments until after supper time and then we could all come back to the courthouse where it's warm and spend the biggest part of the night here in the court house listening to the final arguments?"*

So the judge said yes, he would. So he recessed the court. So every-
body went back to their wagons and got supper, and then about dark,
why then they came back to the court, and it reconvened and they
were just hanging off the rafters in there. Everybody that could get in.
And, of course, the lawyers just went all out 'cause they had a
tremendous audience, you know. But court week was a great source of
entertainment and it was up until the late 1940s.

Or even into the 1990s, when TV put everybody back in the courtroom again.

"The church was your outstanding social

function, because there you met all your

neighbors that you hadn't seen for a week."

The Church as Entertainment

"The young people are about to lonesome to death," a Texas County correspondent wrote to the local newspaper in 1902, "Such a pity the church can't be finished so we can have prayer meeting, Sunday school, and preaching."

Today's Ozarkers, young people and old alike, are much less likely to "lonesome to death," than their turn-of-the-century forebears. Nearly constant entertainment is available through the home TV set. Shopping malls, movie theatres, video arcades, concerts, operas, plays, and a myriad of other distractions are within easy access to all. It was not always so.

Rural Ozarkers of an earlier time had to rely on their own resources and those of their communities for diversion from the difficult and often lonely business of everyday living. Picnics, literaries, pie suppers, barn raisings, quiltings, and other such gatherings were all enjoyable and entertaining. So were religious services. "The church was your outstanding social function," an elderly Douglas County man told me, "because there you met all your neighbors that you hadn't seen for a week."

Early Ozarkers looked to their church for help and guidance, not only about how to make it into the next world, but how to conduct themselves in this one. And the church was never reluctant to give this advice.

In 1896, the Elders of the Church of Christ at Ash Grove published an edict listing activities to be avoided by their followers. "We believe," the Elders wrote,

> that the Bible clearly teaches that the modern dance; card parties and
> card playing, either for amusement or for a wager or prize; theatre
> going; fornication; adultery; stealing; lying; perjury; the use, sale,
> and manufacture of alcoholic spirits as a beverage; betting; covet-

ness; neglect of the worship of the house of the Lord; and all other
disorderly conduct are hurtful and pernicious, both in themselves and
in their consequences.

Some people might say, "What's left?"

One thing that was left was the church itself. Since many churches forbad indulging in a lot of the entertainments and diversions otherwise available, the people turned increasingly to the church itself for entertainment. Good preaching, for example, was greatly appreciated.

Ministers who were eloquent in the pulpit soon acquired a loyal group of admirers. Their sermons were enthusiastically reviewed by parishioner-correspondents who wrote of their performances in glowing terms. "The most brilliant and oratorical sermon that it has been our privilege to hear." And, "An interesting and effective talker, startling at times, but always commanding attention."

The revival, or protracted, meeting was among the most anticipated entertainment events of the year. "I'd give a hunnert dollars right now to go to a real old-fashioned camp meeting for thirty days!" a retired Taney County preacher said longingly.

I was told of one testimony meeting which started one night about a half hour before preaching was to begin at a protracted meeting:

That thing broke loose, and they got that testimony meetin' started,
and it lasted till after two o'clock, and they was thirteen conversions
came out of that testimony. The preacher he couldn't do nothin' with
'em. He tried to stop them, but they wasn't nothin' doin'. They was
testifyin' all over the place.

Baptizings attracted large crowds to riverbanks throughout the Ozarks. Although baptizing was a serious religious rite, there were occasions when the solemnity might be broken. Like the time one baptismal party became entangled in trot lines stretched across the stream. There was excitement at another baptizing when a large hog seized a two-year old child and carried it off some distance. Everything turned out ok, however. The child was rescued unharmed, the hog was shot, and the baptizing went on.

At another baptizing the unrepentant husband of one of the candidates for baptism rode his horse into the stream and attempted to stop the proceedings. It was proudly reported that "Threats of muscular Christianity intervened," and the baptizing continued.

Some river baptizings don't sound very entertaining. A lady down in Wright County told me,

> I was baptized the 22nd day of February. There was snow on the ground and ice on the crick, and they's 33 of us baptized that day, and I walked about as far as from here to the bridge down there just in my sock feet, and they cut the ice and moved the ice back to make room to baptize us, and it didn't make a one of us sick, and there were 33 of us.

And one old woman spoke very scornfully of what she called "Warm Weather Baptists"—people who were converted in the winter time but chose to wait to summer to be baptized. She had no use for warm weather Baptists.

Ozarkers have always loved a good argument.

A true Ozarker will avoid stating his opinion on

a controversial issue until he finds out the

position of a person he has just met,

so he can take the opposite side.

Debate

Back in 1896, patrons of the Lilly School District in Ozark County, became engrossed in the debate topic, "Resolved: That the sun revolves around the earth." The opinion of the community seemed to be pretty well divided on the question, and both sides were well represented in debates at the local school house. As a matter of fact, interest in the subject was so high that a series of debates were held. At the final debate however, the local paper reported, "J. W. Curry made a strong and well defined argument in favor of the affirmative which turned the tide of opinion to a remarkable degree." The decision went to the affirmative.

In Ozark County, the sun does revolve around the earth.

Ozarkers have always loved a good argument. A true Ozarker will avoid stating his opinion on a controversial issue until he finds out the position of a person he has just met, so he can take the opposite side. And we're not surprised to find our man (and it is usually a man) a couple of hours later, in different company, arguing strongly against the position he had only recently supported. The satisfaction of a good verbal contest goes back a long way in the Ozarks.

The Friday Night Literaries held at the local school house in most rural communities, would usually include a debate. And the interests of Ozarkers, if the subjects they debated are any indication, were far from provincial. Current issues were taken up: "Resolved: That absolute free trade would be for the best interests of the American people," "Resolved: That Cuba should be annexed to the United States," and "Resolved: That women should have the right to vote," are examples of turn-of-the-century topics.

Some topics sound quite modern to us. "That foreign immigration should be prohibited, " and "That the public school system as at present conducted is a nuisance and a fraud and should be abolished."

Perhaps the most popular debate topics were the universal and perhaps unresolvable. For example, "That fire is more destructive than water," or "That man will go further for love than for money." Debates on this kind of topic were often humorous, and were often reported in considerable detail by the weekly newspaper correspondents.

The cow vs the sheep held the audience last Friday, verdict for the cow. Next Friday... the subject for debate is the dishrag vs. the broom and the fur will fly as all the distinguished orators have lined up and are consulting ancient and modern history for facts and figures. The writer is on the dishrag side as he has some sad memories of the use and abuse of the broom when wielded by the hands of an irate housewife.

When the literary at Scott school house in Greene County was to debate, "Resolved: That woman is more attracting to the eye of man than monkeys," a correspondent inquired, "Now just how many monkeys will be present at the aforesaid debate to bear witness just how attractive a woman is to a monkey's eye? You should tote fair with the monkeys, gentlemen."

Debate teams were sometimes made up of schoolchildren, but more commonly they were formed of adult members of the community who, in Vance Randolph's words, "Could think up a powerful good speech in a whole week of walkin' down the corn rows."

When a district developed one or more favorite debaters who could be expected to uphold the honor of the society, a challenge was sent to a neighboring community for a meeting of champions. This challenge was sometimes issued through the columns of the local newspaper, as was this one from Seligman: "The question, Resolved: That each man's life is what he makes it, has been debated at almost every school house in the township. Two men, Roller and Murray from Seligman, are ready to meet in debate any other two debaters who may favor the affirmative."

Political questions were debated along sharply partisan lines, and decisions were rendered in the same manner. Brushy Knob Society debated the free-silver issue in 1898: "The affirmative was represented by five Democrats, and the negative by five Republicans. The Republicans tied the silver men up in knots and had them beat from the start," wrote the local correspondent. The vote by the audience was 30 to 8 in favor of the Republican side.

One elderly debater provided his own resolution to a debate when he became offended at the personal remarks of a member of the opposition, picked up the coal-oil lantern that he had brought to the schoolhouse and stalked out of the building. Since the lantern had provided the only light for the debate, the meeting adjourned at once.

And a correspondent wrote: "The question for debate last Saturday night, Resolved, that life is not worth living, was decided in favor of the affirmative which has made us feel so bad that I wasn't able to eat but seven biscuits for breakfast."

Ketchel earned the nickname "The Michigan

Assassin," for his two-handed, brawling style of

fighting. Of his 61 fights, he had lost only four,

and one of those was to Jack Johnson,

the heavyweight champion.

The Ketchel Melodrama:

Act One

The murder trial was the theatrical event of the season. It involved a world famous athlete, a special prosecutor, a colorful defense attorney, and a parade of witnesses. A law officer was accused of prejudice, and there were arguments over jurors.

This particular trial did not take place on the west coast in the 1990s, but in the Missouri Ozarks. The year was 1911.

The murdered man was Stanley Ketchel, the middleweight boxing champion of the world. He was 24 years old and at the height of his career when he was shot in the back with a .22 caliber rifle at a Webster County Ranch.

Ketchel had run away from his Michigan home when he was 12. He greatly admired Jesse James, and soon began carrying a six-shooter in his waistband. Ketchel earned the nickname, "The Michigan Assassin," for his two-handed, brawling style of fighting. Of his 61 fights, he had lost only four, and one of those was to Jack Johnson, the heavyweight champion.

How did a famous boxing champion come to be at a ranch on the Gasconade River? We need to meet another key player in this melodrama, the Ozarks millionaire.

Rollin P. Dickerson was a successful Springfield banker, business man, super patriot, and sports buff. He had been a private in the Spanish-American war, but people called him "Colonel" when they met him walking his pet lion cub on a leather leash. Dickerson owned an 860 acre ranch in Webster County.

In September, 1910, Dickerson went to Grand Rapids, Michigan for a short vacation and fishing trip. When he returned, he brought with him Stanley Ketchel, whose mother was an old friend from Dickerson's boyhood days in

Michigan.

Ketchel wanted to move up to the more prestigious and lucrative heavyweight division. He came to spend some time at Dickerson's ranch, where he would train and add more weight to his 158 pounds. But apparently Ketchel fell in love with the Ozarks. Less than a month after he arrived in Springfield, Ketchel wrote a friend in the Bronx that he had quit the fighting game and was going into the farming business.

To gain experience at this farming business, it was decided that he would manage Dickerson's Webster County ranch. To help Ketchel on the ranch, Dickerson engaged the Spear's employment agency to find a ranch hand and housekeeper.

Walter Dipley was a 23 year old Navy deserter. His common-law wife, Goldie Smith, was 22 and had been living what she described as a "bad life" in Kansas. They had met only a couple of months earlier while visiting relatives in Christian County. Their visiting done, and in need of money, they moved to a boarding house in Springfield. At the Spear's employment agency they learned of an opening for a ranch hand and housekeeper. They were hired.

The principal actors of this melodrama are now together at the ranch. The second scene can begin.

One evening Dipley came in from the fields. He later told the court:

*I seen that there was something wrong with Goldie and I asked her
what was wrong: she said nothing was the matter. I asked her two or
three times.*

Finally, Goldie told Dipley that Ketchel had thrown her on the bed and. as she later testified, "Accomplished the biggest part of what he undertook." To avoid trouble, they decided to leave the ranch the next day.

In the morning, while Goldie fixed Ketchel his breakfast, Dipley went out to feed the horses. When Dipley reentered the house, the trouble began. Dipley described it at the trial:

*[Ketchel] said, "What in hell are you doing around the house at this
time of day; why hain't you out in the field?" I says, "Why, I am not
going out in the field today. I have quit."*

There were more words, and according to Dipley's testimony, Ketchel reached for his six- shooter:

He said, "If you start anything, I will shoot you in two." I grabbed the
little rifle at the corner there. I told him, I says, "Throw up your
hands." He said, "By God, I won't." Then I shot.

Ketchel was mortally wounded. When Dickerson, in Springfield, was notified of the incident, he immediately had the Frisco put together a special train to take him to Webster County. The dying Ketchel was loaded in the baggage car, and the train made its way back to Springfield, with Dickerson, at every stop, offering a $5,000 reward for Dipley dead, "not one cent for him alive."

There are more acts to the melodrama. The trial itself, the hired prosecutor, the picture show, the bounty hunter.

But they must wait for another time.

The Webster County ranch where Ketchel was

killed was owned by Colonel R.P. "Pete"

Dickerson, a wealthy Springfield banker,

pawnbroker, business man, sports

enthusiast, and super-patriot.

The Ketchel Melodrama:

Act Two

In an earlier program I talked about a murder trial regarding a famous athlete. Stanley Ketchel, the middleweight boxing champion of the world was shot and killed at a Webster County ranch in 1910.

The killer was a born loser. His name was Walter Dipley, he had deserted from the United States Navy, and he shot Ketchel in a dispute over Dipley's live-in girl friend, Goldie Smith.

The Webster County ranch where Ketchel was killed was owned by Colonel R. P. "Pete" Dickerson, a wealthy Springfield banker, pawnbroker, business man, sports enthusiast, and super- patriot. Some people felt that he was Ketchel's natural father, although Dickerson consistently denied it.

When people at the ranch called Dickerson in Springfield to tell him Ketchel had been shot, Dickerson immediately ordered the Frisco Railroad to assemble a special train to go to Conway, the nearest town to the ranch, to pick up the wounded Ketchel.

When Dickerson got to the ranch, he dashed into the room where Ketchel lay. "Stanley, speak to me. How did this happen?" "I was sitting at the kitchen table," Ketchel whispered, "and I was shot in the back."

"Get the woman too," Ketchel added, "for she robbed me." Both Dipley and Goldie would later deny taking any money from Ketchel.

Dickerson became very excited, and dashed from the house offering a reward of $5,000 for Dipley. This was an offer that he would repeat many times, usually with the stipulation that the reward would be paid for Dipley dead, and "not one cent for him alive!"

The assembled doctors decided that Ketchel's wound was fatal, and that he should be taken to the hospital in Springfield.

After giving the order to get Ketchel ready for the trip back to Springfield, Dickerson went back outside. This time he told the people to find Dipley, to shoot first and then yell "halt!" He wanted Dipley's head or arm to hang on his living room wall.

At Conway, and at other stops on the train trip back, Dickerson repeated to the crowds his offer of $5,000 for Dipley dead. News of the huge reward spread quickly by word of mouth and the telephone. Practically everyone in the county soon heard of the reward for the man who shot Ketchel.

Meanwhile, the man who had shot Ketchel was making his way along the railroad tracks toward Marshfield, the county seat, to surrender to the Sheriff. Dipley later explained that he stopped and rested a lot, so that by the evening of the shooting, he was still some five miles from Marshfield.

He stopped at the farm house of Thomas Hoggard and asked to spend the night. He was from Christian County, he said, and was hunting some stray horses. After supper, Dipley went upstairs to the spare bedroom to go to sleep.

Two of Hoggard's children were sent over to a neighbor's house, Zib Murphy, to borrow some molasses. When they told Murphy about the stranger spending the night, Murphy wondered if he might be the one everybody was looking for. Zib then spent the entire night shuttling back and forth in the neighborhood, making many telephone calls, and trying to get a description of the wanted man. At four o'clock in the morning, Zib went over to Thomas's place, and the two of them set up, trying to figure out what to do.

About six-thirty that morning, Joe Hoggard appeared at the farm. Joe was Thomas Hoggard's brother, and had come over to get Thomas to help him drag off a dead horse. Thomas and Zib filled Joe in about the stranger upstairs. The wanted man had tatoos on his arm. They didn't know about the stranger.

Joe, always a man of action, took charge. Brother Thomas later described in court what happened:

> Joe rolled off of his horse and came in the kitchen where the stair
> steps started up. Joe walked on to the stairway and nodded to Murphy
> and I to follow him and of course we followed him; and he [Dipley]
> was sitting on the bed. Mr. Murphy and my brother Joe demanded to

see his arm: of course his arm filled the descriptions we had got and
my brother told him to consider himself under arrest.

The three men walked Dipley a mile and a half into Niangua, where they bought him breakfast while they waited for a rig to be prepared. They then took Dipley into Marshfield where they turned him over to Sheriff Cobe Fields.

Dipley would be tried for murder, and the three who captured him, Zib Murphy and the Hoggard brothers, would apply to Colonel Dickerson for the $5000 reward money. That would result in still another trial, which we'll talk about on the next White River Journal.

At Marshfield, Dickerson, from the train, make

his offer for "the dead body of the man who shot

Stanley Ketchel." Someone in the crowd asked

how much he would give for him living. "Nothing

at all," Dickerson replied, "I want him dead."

The Ketchel Melodrama:

Act Three

In an earlier episode of White River Journal, I talked about how, in 1910, a drifter named Walter Dipley shot and killed Stanley Ketchel, the middleweight boxing champion of the world, at a Webster County ranch. Ketchel was the protégée of a wealthy Springfield business man, Colonel R. P. Dickerson, who owned the ranch.

At Dipley's trial, Dickerson personally hired a prominent attorney to serve as special prosecutor, and invited the Webster County Sheriff to a private showing of a movie featuring Ketchel's fight with the heavyweight champion, Jack Johnson. Dickerson was taking no chances that Dipley would escape conviction.

But Dickerson would himself become involved in a trial, and would be defended by the same attorney he had employed to prosecute Dipley. Here's what happened.

When he was notified in Springfield of the shooting, Dickerson hired a train to go to Conway, the nearest railroad town to the ranch, to pick up the mortally wounded Ketchel. By the time Dickerson got there, Dipley had already left the ranch, walking toward Marshfield, the county seat. After seeing the dying Ketchel, the excitable Dickerson dashed from the ranch house encouraging everyone within earshot to go after and capture the killer, offering a reward of $5,000.

It was an offer Dickerson would make several times. At Marshfield, Dickerson, from the train, made his offer for "the dead body of the man who shot Stanley Ketchel." Someone in the crowd asked how much he would give for him living. "Nothing at all," Dickerson replied, "I want him dead."

Several of Dickerson's expressions hint at his desire to have Dipley killed rather than captured: "He is armed – bring him in dead." And "Shoot him first and cry 'halt' afterwards." Word of the extravagant reward soon spread.

Meanwhile, Dipley was making his deliberate way toward Marshfield. He stopped at the farm house of Thomas Hoggard, and asked to spend the night. With the rural hospitality of the time, he was given supper and shown to the upstairs spare bedroom.

In the last White River Journal, I described how Thomas Hoggard, his brother Joe, and a neighbor, Zib Murphy, aroused Dipley early the next morning, determined to their satisfaction that he was the wanted man, and escorted him into Marshfield, where they turned him over to the Sheriff. Dipley gave them no trouble. He was tried for murder, and convicted.

A few weeks after the murder, the three men who had brought Dipley in, the Hoggard brothers and Zib Murphy, called on Dickerson in his Springfield office to collect the reward. Dickerson refused. He explained why:

> They came in. I says, "Gentlemen, what can I do for you?" They says, "We come up to see about that reward for capturing Dipley." I says, "I never offered any reward for him alive. I offered it for him dead."

Zib Murphy added:

> He said a right smart more. He said he would have liked for us to have shot him; just shot him a little. Just shot him up enough so he would have to suffer a week or so.

After the men complained that they had been out about $3.50 in expenses, Dickerson offered to give them $15. You can split it three ways, he said. Dickerson wrote them a check which, he later maintained, was in full settlement of their claim. When they asked him for more, he refused. "He just shut the window down right in front of us," Thomas Hoggard complained, "and that was the last I saw of him."

So the three sued in Greene County Circuit Court to collect the $5,000 reward.

Five leading Ozarks lawyers were involved: three for the plaintiffs, two for Dickerson (one of whom was Roscoe Patterson, the private special prosecutor). Dickerson's defense was threefold: 1) he did make an offer of a reward, but that it was for the murderer dead, not one cent for him alive; 2) all offers were emotionally made and he was so excited he didn't intend to contract with anyone and, 3) furthermore, the plaintiffs accepted the $15 check in full settlement of their claim.

The jury found the plaintiffs were entitled to receive the reward of $5,000, plus interest, a total award of $5, 612.50.

Dickerson appealed. The Greene County Court of Appeals upheld the award of the lower court, reasoning that Dickerson's offer of a reward would require the person earning it to commit a crime. Judge Sturgis wrote, "We think that an offer to pay a reward for a man or for his capture should be taken as meaning for his capture in a lawful manner."

The court also agreed that the check for $15 was not a payment of reward, but was to cover expenses only.

Three years and seven months after the Hoggard brothers and Zib Murphy locked Walter Dipley in the county jail at Marshfield, they could at last collect their reward.

Ozarks baseball games were more than

casual athletic contests: on the conduct and

performance of a team rode the pride

and prestige of an entire community.

Baseball

Ozarkers have always taken their baseball games seriously. In early autumn of 1892, the Mountain Grove baseball club notified the Ava club that it would be "unable" to play a scheduled game. After announcing this fact, the editor of the Ava newspaper wrote what started as a good- natured jibe. It quickly developed, however, into a bitter harangue against the Mountain Grove club. Of the cancellation he said:

> *That is a wise step. They have outlived their usefulness, they have exhausted their "hoodoo," have met and vanquished, cheated and bluffed several amateur clubs, had the egotism to cross bats with ball players and were used as mops, chewed up and spit out and in the vernacular of the day discovered that they were "not in it." Don't submit your citizens to any further humiliation, gag yourselves, take your ball bats and herd geese, and the first man that pokes his slimy head through the green scum of obscurity and yells "baseball," make an angel of him on the spot.*

And they call baseball a game!

It's obvious that Ozarks baseball games were more than casual athletic contests: on the conduct and performance of a team rode the pride and prestige of an entire community.

As a matter of fact, being a spectator at a turn-of-the-century Ozarks baseball game was not necessarily a passive occupation. In 1902, in the eighth inning of a game between Lebanon and Marshfield, the umpire called a Lebanon player out. Although the game was being played in Webster County, home turf for Marshfield, the angry Lebanon fans poured onto the field. and, according to the

Marshfield paper:

> *For half an hour they indulged in the most violent, abusive language*
> *to the umpire and visiting team, and so great was their rage that for*
> *the space of nearly half an hour there was imminent danger of a riot.*

The newspaper credited the Lebanon team with the "utmost sincerity," but suggested, slyly, "If one has the desire to see a tough crowd that does not know the meaning of the word courtesy, he has only to go to Lebanon to find it."

A Gainesville umpire protected himself from over-zealous fans and angry players by wearing two horse pistols (the writer called them "mountain howitzers"), buckled under his arms. In spite of this, the West Plains team protested a decision early in the game, and, according to the Gainesville correspondent, "kept on the kicking act through the game, proving they could out kick an Ozark County mule."

Occasionally, two clubs would meet in a spirit of peace, harmony, and sportsmanship. When this occurred, it was reported in the newspapers as a rarity.

The most colorful team that played in the Ozarks was a traveling professional club, the Nebraska Indians, who were well promoted before they played the local clubs. The fans were promised that the players retain the customs of their "fierce ancestors," and that they "refuse to go into a game without donning their war paint and chanting their favorite war songs. They carry their own wigwams."

Such publicity drew large crowds eager for a look at the ferocious warriors in action. People in at least one town were disappointed. The Ava editor reported that "there were only two that looked anything like Indians. A majority of them were white men." Although it was a great game and well worth going to see (the Ava team won), the failure to produce nine full-blood Indians as promised lessened the theatrical impact of the afternoon.

Baseball playing on Sunday caused distress in some communities. A Houston correspondent admonished ball players:

> *The Lord made this world in six days and on the seventh day he rested*
> *and while you are playing ball you are not observing the Sabbath as*
> *the Bible says you should. What a beautiful old world this would be if*
> *there were no such doings.*

In 1905 the Missouri legislature failed to pass a bill that would have prohibited Sunday baseball. The Sunday games continued, and the crowds continued to watch and participate both vocally and physically in this dramatic sport. After the first five years of the new century, however, some of the gusto and frontier spirit seemed to fade away.

As the games became less important, some of the more partisan voices were stilled. Voices like that of a Salem, Arkansas editor who, after his club was defeated by a Gainesville team in 1895, had written: "If we were forced to choose between Hades and Ozark County, Missouri as our future destination, we would study long and loud before making the choice, for we figure the odds are rather in favor of Hades…"

Christmas Tree programs were held in churches,

schoolhouses, courthouses, or any meeting place

big enough to hold the large number of people

who attended this popular event.

Community Christmas Trees

There are signs of Christmas all over the Ozarks.

No spaces in the mall parking lots. A Christmas tree vendor on every corner, and the gift catalogues stuffing the mailbox leaving little room for the Christmas cards.

Communities have been staging Christmas parades, complete with floats, antique cars, and marching bands. Santa Claus, Miss Merrie Christmas, and the Nativity share featured billing. And lights! Each year more and more communities join in the Festival of Lights, and try to outdo each other with stars, snowflakes, angels and alligators, and miles of lights enticing visitors to wend their ways slowly through an electric maze, oohing and awing at the beauty and spectacle.

In the early Ozarks, many small towns also celebrated Christmas as a community, but in quite a different way. Early Ozarks residents seldom had Christmas trees in their homes, as we now do. Instead, they joined in a community project, commonly called the "Christmas Tree." Christmas Tree programs were held in churches, schoolhouses, courthouses, or any meeting place big enough to hold the large number of people who attended this popular event

These community Christmas Trees usually featured a literary or musical program, and had, as a climactic event, the revealing of a large Christmas tree. The tree would, of course, be handsomely decorated with strings of tinsel, popcorn, and cranberries, and lighted with candles. Presents hung from its branches and were piled on the floor beneath. The editor of an Ozark County paper in 1893 squeezed his way through "a great throng of humanity," into the Christmas Tree at Gainesville. Of the large cedar tree he wrote, "Its dazzling beauty and splendor as it met the gaze and admiration of thousands of eyes was something never to be forgotten."

As the time came for the presents to be distributed, Santa Claus made his appearance. He would hold each present, call out the recipient's name, and make witty remarks for the amusement and delight of the audience. In addition to the regular presents, gag gifts were hung from the tree limbs, giving Santa material for extemporizing at the expense of the recipients. At a Galena Christmas Tree, these gag gifts included a diaper for a newly married couple and a stick of wood for the president of the local "never-sweat" club (so he could be assured of some holiday warmth without having to exert himself).

In many communities, local merchants subscribed to a fund to assure that every child would receive a present, and collections were taken up for special gifts, like the $21.25 suit of clothes placed on the tree for a Mount Vernon minister.

The program that preceded the distribution of presents was short, for people were eager to get on to the more exciting business ahead. At a church Christmas Tree, the children's choir often presented a simple cantata or play.

Although the Christmas tree received generally favorable acceptance throughout the Ozarks, there were some who disapproved of the custom perhaps because they saw the tree as a pagan symbol. Whether it was to appease these dissenters, or simply because they wanted to provide a more elaborate stage setting, some communities distributed presents not from a Christmas tree but from some other decorative device. A few of these settings were a Jacob's ladder, a snow house, an arch, a windmill, an old log church, a Christmas wheel, and a fairy garden. The New Church at Exeter struck a patriotic theme with a setting representing the battleship Maine, complete with sailor boys.

Much to the distress of the good people of the community, the Christmas Trees sometimes attracted elements who were intent on creating their own brand of Christmas cheer. Here are three typical incidents reported in the weekly newspapers of the day:

> *We understand there was a very lively time at the Christmas Tree at Henry schoolhouse. A few fights, several eyes in mourning, and lots of tanglefoot.*

*An old quarrel was the trouble which was renewed when they met at
the Christmas Tree, and Levi shot at Elmer but missed him, no damage done.*

*One man present said that he was going to kiss every lady present,
but was promptly knocked out by one of the ladies.*

And then this laconic observation:

*We had right good order until it broke and then there was a right
smart of shooting took place.*

Such conduct was not universal, and a Christian County correspondent wrote
a glowing epilogue to the Christmas Tree in these words:

*After all the presents had been distributed, the people started for
their homes feeling life is not made up altogether of trials and trou
bles, and with a hope that they might be permitted to meet together on
many more similar occasions.*

There seemed to be only three requisites for an

Ozarks picnic: a good spring, plenty of shade,

and an excuse. The first two were to be found in

abundance, and the Fourth of July presented one

of the best reasons for whole communities to get

together for a grand patriotic celebration.

Fourth of July Picnics

Early day Ozarkers had an enormous capacity for simply enjoying each other. They were forced by circumstances of geography to live a more or less isolated existence, so they welcomed any opportunity to meet socially with friends and neighbors. Picnics presented one of these times.

There seemed to be only three requisites for an Ozarks picnic: a good spring, plenty of shade, and an excuse. The first two were to be found in abundance, and the Fourth of July presented one of the best reasons for whole communities to get together for a grand patriotic celebration.

These "jubilations" ranged from simple basket dinners and sociability to elaborate all-day programs with parades, orations, and fireworks.

The larger picnics often featured a parade that began the day's festivities. Country people rose early to do their morning chores so they could be in town to see the spectacle, often arriving as early as sunrise. A Fourth of July parade was made up of whatever marching and riding elements could be persuaded to participate—floats, sponsored by merchants; bicyclists; wagons and buggies; and men and women on horseback added to the color and excitement of the event. A band, of course, was nearly indispensable.

The grand theme of Fourth of July celebrations in the Ozarks was patriotism. "The American Eagle will spread his wings and soar aloft over the summits of the Ozarks," wrote Truman Powell to the *Stone County Oracle* in 1904. "Patriotism should be taught to the rising generation," he went on, "and the Fourth of July is the time to do it." To accomplish this end, every celebration worth its name included someone reciting the Declaration of Independence, as well as a star- spangled assortment of orators.

It was a great honor to be chosen to read the Declaration of Independence from the platform. The audience listened to the words of that document with a reverence usually reserved for the reading of Scripture. The prime requisite of such a performer was that he or she be able to speak in a loud, clear voice that could be understood by all within earshot. There was no electronic amplification, of course, and the speakers had to compete with the noise of the circle swing and the barking of the lemonade vendors.

Every decent Fourth of July picnic had to have at least one featured orator who would deliver a long-winded, flag-waving speech in a style known as "spreading the eagle." One such speaker was described as being "as eloquent as he is loud, as logical as he is lengthy, and as entertaining as he is interesting."

There was always food, of course. Often, families placed the food they had brought on a large table, and the resulting spread was shared by all. At Alton, in 1896, there was a feast when two beeves, eleven sheep, and six hogs were killed and barbecued.

Circle swings, forerunners to modern merry-go-rounds, were regular features at the picnics. The first swings were propelled by manpower or horsepower. Lemonade stands did a thriving business, and were usually the only concessions on the grounds. Greased pole climbing, foot races of every kind, bicycle races, and egg races were standard items on most programs. Another favorite, the tug of war, was given added interest at Ava in 1910 when twelve country women were pitted against twelve town ladies. There were prizes for both men and women in the hitching and harnessing contest at Ozark in 1901.

The special attraction of the afternoon's entertainment was often a baseball game. The folks at Ava, however, must have gotten tired of cheering before the afternoon was over on the Fourth of July, 1892. The Ava boys swamped visiting Bryant Creek, 63 to 5.

Attendance prizes were awarded at most picnics to those who met certain qualifications: Oldest married couple, laziest man, largest married couple. At Galena there were prizes for bringing the largest number of people from the country in one wagon (the winner brought 13), to the man who had cast the most votes for president (15), and to the woman having the largest number of children present (eight children, awarded 25 pounds of flour).

After the orators had finished and the prizes had been awarded and darkness had fallen, there would be fireworks, but many of the country folk could not stay. An Ozark County country correspondent summed it up: "As the shadows lengthened in the grove, remembering the weary miles back home, the crowd started breaking up, tired but very happy. Some of their friends they met today they would not see again 'till next Fourth of July. This was 'the end of a perfect day,' and one long to be remembered."